Financial Fitness

Balancing Health and Wealth for Entrepreneurs & All Workers

By Bradley R. Edmonds

Even though he obtained the level of wealth he so desperately desired, acquired plenty of cash, a mansion, automobiles, and plenty of people to command, he still felt robbed because his body and health began to deteriorate and he had to visit the doctor more frequently, as if the doctor's office were his second office. Raphael grew up in a very poor family where his next meal was considered a miracle. He and his family view education as an impossibility. Raphael was raised in a family of five(5), consisting of a mother and father, two (2) boys, three (3) girls, and five(5) children. He was the oldest of five children and came from a family that was all too familiar with the harsh realities of poverty. Their love for one another was their greatest treasure, and despite the challenges they faced, their spirits remained unwavering. Maria and Carlos, Raphael's parents, put up a lot of effort to support their offspring. Carlos worked as a construction worker, and the years of arduous labor in the sweltering sun had left his hands calloused. Maria worked odd jobs as a cleaning lady and even volunteered at the neighborhood market; her worn-out apron was a symbol of her unwavering resolve. Raphael learned the importance of each meal while he was a child. The family sat around the weathered oak table, laughing and telling stories as they cherished each piece of the modest rice and beans that had filled their house. Raphael's parents always made the food seem like a feast despite the little servings, showing their kids that contentment could be found in even the most modest things. Raphael's world broadened through books he took out from the neighborhood library. He envisioned amazing adventures, went to distant locations, and dreamed of a better future with each page he turned. His best times were when he could read to his younger siblings, Mateo and Amelia, and weave stories that would distract them from the difficulties of their daily lives. Raphael became more and more determined to end the cycle of poverty as the years went by. He did well in school and frequently stayed up late to study in the library's quiet areas. He was aware that education was the key to a better life and the opportunity to free his family from their struggles. Even though they were unable to assist with his studies, his parents never-endingly encouraged him and consistently expressed delight in his accomplishments. A lovely instructor named Ms. Rodriguez noticed Raphael's dedication and saw potential in him. She gave him advice. She assisted him with his scholarship applications and put him in touch with mentors who could give him perspective on the wider world. Raphael was able to get a scholarship to a prominent university with the assistance of Ms. Rodriguez and his family's steadfast affection. One of the toughest things Raphael has ever done was leave his family behind. He relocated to the city and learned to live in a setting that was completely foreign to him. Even though his family broke his heart, he was determined to make them proud. He worked part-time jobs to pay his bills and send some money home while pursuing his education with tremendous dedication.

Raphael put forth a lot of effort and pursued achievement with unyielding tenacity. He sought possibilities, ascended corporate ladders, and made investments in businesses that offered lucrative returns. Boardrooms, meetings, and negotiations dominated his life as he relentlessly pursued financial success. Raphael remained true to his heritage. He assisted in remodeling his childhood home to make it a cozy and welcoming space. To give his siblings the opportunity he worked so hard to secure, he continued to finance their schooling.

Raphael accumulated a fortune that appeared to be beyond his wildest fantasies as the years went by. He had all the material things he had ever wanted, including a large mansion, fine automobiles, and other stuff. Even yet, he was unable to hide the toll his lifestyle was having on his health behind the sparkling façade of his success.

Unrelenting stress, poor dietary choices, and neglected exercise had slowly deteriorated his health. Raphael had become richer, but he had also become sicker. A trip to the doctor revealed the shocking fact that his body was suffering as a result of the disregard he had shown it. Raphael was presented with a decision he had never considered, and he concluded that wealth was nothing without health. His most pressing need was now the precise thing he had compromised his health for. He suddenly found himself in a situation he could never have anticipated, needing to utilize his newfound fortune to reclaim the vigor he had lost. Raphael set out on a different path because he was determined to undo the harm he had caused. He invested the same efforts in his health that he had earlier put into building a fortune by hiring a personal trainer and nutritionist. The process was difficult and demanded patience and dedication that he had not needed in his quest for wealth. Raphael learned what true prosperity meant as he gradually gave up unhealthy habits and adopted a more balanced way of life. It wasn't only about having enough money; it was also about having the energy to enjoy life's little joys. His new treasures were going for a stroll in the park, laughing with friends, and living each moment to the fullest.

Disclaimer

This book, "Financial Fitness: Balancing Health and Wealth for entrepreneurs and all workers," contains information that is solely meant to be used for general education and counseling. The information in the book is based on the author's research, experience, and current information. It is not meant to be a replacement for qualified financial, medical, or legal advice. To resolve their unique financial, medical, or legal problems, readers are recommended to speak with qualified specialists such as financial advisors, doctors, or lawyers. Any actions taken by readers as a result of the information contained in this book are not the responsibility of the author or publisher.

Every attempt has been made to guarantee the trustworthiness and accuracy of the information offered. However, the content's accuracy, completeness, or fitness for any particular purpose is not warranted or guaranteed by the author or publisher. It is the responsibility of the reader to check the accuracy of the information and make judgments based on their own situation.

The use of or reliance on the information in this book may have direct or indirect repercussions, losses, or damages for which the author and publisher expressly disclaim any liability or obligation.

When applying the concepts and tactics covered in this book to their personal financial and health situations, readers must use prudence and good judgment. Your unique situation can call for specialized solutions, thus this book is meant to be a broad reference rather than to offer specific guidance.

Table of content

Introduction

The pursuit of financial success has become of utmost importance in the complicated and constantly changing environment of the modern world. Financial health is about creating a condition of fiscal well-being where you have control over your finances, can fulfill your financial goals, and most importantly, can feel peace of mind. It's not only about collecting cash. In **"Financial Fitness: Balancing Health and Wealth for Entrepreneurs & All Workers,"** we go on a trip that explores the worlds of financial knowledge, balanced living, and how these two seemingly separate elements of life are fundamentally interrelated.

We are used to establishing lofty goals and working incredibly hard to attain them as businesspeople, professionals, and people who like to get things done, but what if there was an alternative route, one that brought about not only material success but also good health, emotional fortitude, and a sense of direction? What if we could achieve financial success without compromising our health, and vice versa? We examine the complex relationship between our financial situation and our physical health in the pages that follow. We explore the fundamental relationship between the two and learn that taking care of both facets of our lives is necessary for obtaining true success.

"Financial Fitness" leads you on a journey of self-discovery through interesting anecdotes, helpful counsel, and doable techniques. You'll discover how to:

Financial health involves more than just accumulating money. You are in a condition of financial well-being when you have the information, resources, and self-control to handle your money well. Setting and accomplishing financial objectives, responsible debt management, long-term investing, and protecting your financial stability from unforeseen setbacks are all important. Financial fitness enables you to make wise financial decisions regardless of the state of the economy and is a lifelong path rather than a destination.

According to a proverb, "health is wealth." Your financial health and your physical and mental well-being are intricately and profoundly related. Your general health can be significantly impacted by the stress of financial issues, which can cause physical diseases like insomnia, anxiety, and even physical ills. On the other hand, failing to take care of your bodily needs may prevent you from putting up the effort and concentration needed to pursue financial success. As true wealth is measured not just in cash but also in energy, happiness, and quality of life, this book emphasizes the need to strike a balance between your financial and physical health.

Your full guide to achieving financial success while keeping a healthy and fulfilling lifestyle is "Financial Fitness: Balancing Health and Wealth for Entrepreneurs & All Workers". In recognition of the particular difficulties they have managing the demands of entrepreneurship, personal finances, and well-being, this book is written exclusively for business owners who work 9 to 5 and shift employees.

In the chapters that follow, we'll examine useful techniques for determining your current financial condition, setting realistic financial objectives, and developing a long-term budget. Balance Your Life's Budget: Learn how financial decisions affect your health and well-being so that you may make decisions that are consistent with your values and objectives.

Consider the value of physical and mental wellness as the cornerstone of long-term prosperity by investing in your health. Discover how making health investments pays off in all facets of life.

Develop Financial Resilience: Learn how to strengthen your finances so that you can withstand life's financial storms without jeopardizing your well-being.

Discover Your Purpose: Recognize the part that passion and purpose play in your financial and personal path, and how they can result in a richer and more fulfilling life. You will gain the knowledge necessary to make wise financial decisions for both your professional and personal lives as we dig into the worlds of investments, risk management, and retirement planning.

However, this book covers more than simply financial terms. Additionally, it stresses how important your physical health, mental health, and work-life balance are to your financial success. You'll learn how to make thoughtful food choices to fuel your daily trip, include exercise in your daily routine, and optimize your workspace for productivity.

By the time you get to the last chapter, you'll not only have the information and resources you need to further your financial objectives, but you'll also have a deeper understanding of the holistic approach to wealth and well-being. Welcome to "Financial Fitness: Balancing Health and Wealth for Entrepreneurs & All Workers" - a guide to a more prosperous and satisfying existence. Join us as we investigate the relationship between health and money and set out on a route to long-term success as we go on this transforming adventure. It's time to rethink what success means and to create a life that is not just financially prosperous but also abundant in health, joy, and fulfillment.

Chapter 1

Understanding your financial health

Raphael understood his financial situation, he knew that with the way things are in his family he can only dream but not having it.

He had to assess His current financial situation, set a goal, creat a budget and started working towards it

This whole chapter explain deeply how you can assess your current financial situation, setting a financial goal, having a plan that will lead to a solid financial health.

Chapter One

Understanding Your Financial Health:

Knowing your existing financial situation is the first step toward financial success and the delicate balancing act between riches and well-being. You must first assess your position in the huge ocean of personal finance before you can guide your financial ship in the direction of your goal. This chapter explores five underlying principles:

1. Examining your present financial situation

You need to be aware of your starting place before you can plot your path to financial success. Examining your income, expenses, assets, and liabilities in detail is necessary to assess your present financial condition. Here are some practical tips for evaluating your financial situation:

A. Income: To start, figure out how much money you make each month from all sources, including your employment, side hustles, investments, and any other income sources. This sum is the basis of your financial strategy.

B. Expenses: Carefully monitor your monthly outlays. This covers both recurring costs like rent or mortgage payments as well as sporadic costs like food, entertainment, and transportation. Financial control depends on knowing where your money is going.

C. Resources Make a list of your possessions, including personal property, real estate, investments, and savings accounts. These are the tools that can help you achieve your financial objectives.

D. obligations: On the other hand, list your obligations, such as unpaid loans, credit card bills, and mortgages. Understanding your debts is essential for managing your debt and making sound financial decisions.

E. Net Worth: To determine your net worth, divide your whole assets by your total liabilities. This number offers a quick overview of your total financial situation.

You'll be able to see your financial strengths and shortcomings more clearly once you've evaluated your present financial condition. This information serves as the foundation for creating attainable financial objectives.

2. Setting financial goals

Your route to financial success is guided by your financial goals. They give you inspiration and direction, enabling you to make well-informed financial choices. Here's how to create sensible financial objectives:

A. Short-term Goals: These are objectives you hope to accomplish in the next one to three years. The creation of an emergency fund, the elimination of high-interest debts, and vacation savings are a few examples.

B. Medium-term Objectives: These are targets you hope to hit in the next three to five years. Examples could be beginning a new business, saving for a down payment on a house, or paying for your child's school.

C. Long-term Goals: These are the overarching objectives that stretch beyond the first five years. Major life events like retirement or leaving a financial legacy for your family are frequently involved.

D. SMART (specific, measurable, attainable, relevant, and time-bound) objectives Make sure your objectives fit these requirements. You can stay accountable by being clear about your goals, tracking your development, making sure they are realistic and applicable to your life, and setting deadlines.

E. Prioritization: When you have several goals, rank them in order of significance and urgency. You can better allocate your resources as a result.

Aim to achieve your financial objectives. They ought to be compatible with your beliefs, goals, and environment. Setting specific objectives provides your financial journey direction and enables you to track your success as you go.

The chapters that follow will cover practical actions to take control of your financial future as well as strategies for developing a budget and financial plan that are in line with your goals. The cornerstones of your path to financial success are knowing your financial situation and establishing clear goals; they will open the door to more money and well-being.

We've already started on the essential steps of evaluating our existing financial condition and defining specific, well-defined financial goals in our quest for financial fitness. Let's now go more deeply into the following crucial elements of this journey:

3. Making a financial plan and budget

It's like having a GPS for your financial journey to have a clear financial blueprint. Your navigational tools, a budget, and a financial plan can help you stay on track as you work toward your financial objectives.

A. Budgeting is the process of creating a thorough plan that details your income and expenses over a predetermined period, usually a month. It serves as a guide for how you should allocate your resources to achieve your financial goals. Here are some tips for making an efficient budget:

Income: Include all of your income sources, including your job, side businesses, and any passive income. Sort your spending into fixed (such as utilities, rent, or a mortgage), as well as variable (such as grocery and entertainment) categories. Set aside a portion of your income for savings, taking into account both short- and long-term objectives. Make sure to account for emergency fund contributions in your spending plan.

B. Financial Plan: Your goals, budget, investments, and a schedule for reaching your objectives are all part of a financial plan, which is a more comprehensive strategy. It takes care of both immediate and long-term financial requirements. Your financial strategy must incorporate:

Develop a plan for how you will invest your money to meet your financial objectives while minimizing risk and maximizing after-tax returns. Plan out your retirement savings and investments, and ensure you have the right insurance to safeguard your financial security in the event of unforeseen circumstances.

4. Keeping track of your expenses

Your ability to keep to your budget determines how effective it is. There are several applications and programs available to help you track your spending automatically. Keeping track of your expenses is a vital habit that makes sure your financial plan stays on track. These tools group your spending into several categories so you can see exactly where your money is going.

No matter how little the transaction, keep the receipts for all of your purchases, and if there isn't a recipe, note the price spent as well as what it was. This is particularly useful for figuring out where you might be overpaying.

Schedule some time every week or month to examine your spending and gauge how it stacks up against your plan. To account for any changes in your financial condition, adjust your budget as necessary.

5. Establishing a Reserve Fund

The creation of an emergency fund is one of the fundamental cornerstones of financial fitness. Unexpected expenses might rapidly stop your financial progress because life is unpredictable. An emergency fund provides a safety net, guaranteeing that you can weather financial storms without resorting to debt or derailing your financial ambitions.

How Much to Save: Aim to accumulate at least three to six months' worth of living expenses in your emergency fund. Given the erratic nature of income, business owners might be wise to have a larger emergency reserve. Create monthly automatic contributions to your emergency fund. Consider it an expense that cannot be changed.

We will examine other methods for controlling debt, making good investments, and safeguarding your financial future in the subsequent chapters. Keep in mind that getting financially fit is a marathon, not a sprint. You're laying the groundwork for a financially stable and prosperous future by making a budget and financial plan, keeping meticulous records of your spending, and setting aside money for emergencies. But let's first discuss the reasons for our actions before moving on.

Chapter 2

Why do you venture in to business or work

Are this one of the reasons?

1. Pursuit of independence
2. Financial Aspirations
3. Innovation and creativity
4. Passion and Purpose
5. Flexibility and work life balance
6. Legacy and impact
7. Navigating market gap
8. Overcoming challenge
9. Desire for Growth

There is always a reason to why we do the things we do. Raphael knew that his home was poor and he needed to get himself and his family out of the present condition.

Chapters Two

what drives people to start businesses

The act of starting a business stands as a magnificent thread in the tapestry of human aspirations, sewn with hopes for independence, riches, and influence. The decision to start a business is the result of a complicated interplay between one's own goals, the state of the economy, and the need for change. When we examine the reasons why people start businesses, we find a rich tapestry of factors that have influenced economies and industries around the world.

1. The desire for independence.

Many entrepreneurial endeavors are driven by a desire for independence. The urge to become one's boss and escape the constraints of conventional work is a strong motivator. Entrepreneurs want to manage their futures, make choices that are in line with their vision, and feel in charge of their careers.

Untold numbers of people are drawn to the path of entrepreneurship by the desire for freedom. It is a fundamental drive that encompasses the desire for independence, freedom, and control over one's fate. This goal is in line with the fundamental human desire to defy social conventions and live a life that is consistent with one's ideals and goals.

The freedom that business offers is one of its most alluring features. Working in traditional employment frequently entails deferring to the judgment of others, complying with established procedures, and operating within predetermined frameworks. However, business owners savor the chance to choose their path. They are free to make decisions that have a direct impact on their enterprises, such as those regarding product offerings, pricing, marketing techniques, and corporate culture. Entrepreneurs are empowered by this ability to experiment, change course, and develop without being constrained by hierarchical clearances. Entrepreneurs frequently look for flexibility that fits their particular working habits. Those who thrive in various circumstances may find the strict schedules and stuffy offices of traditional occupations to be oppressive. Flexible work schedules, remote work choices, and the freedom to customize one's workspace are all made possible by entrepreneurship. This flexibility promotes a healthier work-life balance by not just accommodating individual preferences but also improving productivity and well-being.

Entrepreneurs frequently strive for independence out of a desire to defy social conventions and expectations. Entrepreneurial endeavors provide an alternative to the well-traveled path by enabling people to explore unexplored ground and create their own stories. Those who are compelled to create their own identities and challenge accepted notions of success can relate to this escape from conformity. Although there are risks associated with being an entrepreneur, the appeal of seeing the fruits of one's labor is a powerful motivator. The freedom to take measured risks offers a chance to question the current quo and possibly experience unheard-of success. For those prepared to handle the difficulties of entrepreneurship, the potential for achieving financial independence and professional distinction can be a strong motivator.

Entrepreneurial independence also involves achieving one's personal goals. To follow their passions, live by their principles, and find purpose in their job, many people are drawn to entrepreneurial endeavors. A regular job's security may not even come close to comparing to the sense of fulfillment that comes from producing something original and significant.
Independent business owners frequently have long-term goals that go beyond short-term success.

They are driven to start businesses that have a long-lasting influence because they want to leave a legacy that will endure after they are gone. This legacy is evidence of their independence, tenacity, and capacity to shape their environment.

The need for independence attracts many to start their businesses. It captures the need for freedom, adaptability, and the capacity to direct one's course. Entrepreneurs are motivated by a deep need to defy expectations, shape their destinies, and make a lasting impact on the world, and they accept the challenges, risks, and rewards that come with this pursuit. This drive for independence not only changes the lives of entrepreneurs but also stimulates invention, economic expansion, and industry development.

2. monetary aspirations

One of the main drivers of commercial endeavors is the appeal of financial success. In addition to securing their financial futures, entrepreneurs hope to build riches that will help their communities and families. Strong inducements that stoke entrepreneurial fantasies include the opportunity for considerable wealth creation and great returns on investment. Many business initiatives are propelled by strong financial aspirations. The temptation of financial success is an all-pervasive inducer of creativity, risk-taking, and arduous effort. Entrepreneurs are attracted to the idea of wealth creation not just for their benefit but also to safeguard their futures, provide for their families, and give back to their communities. Let's examine how aspirations for money are crucial to entrepreneurship:

The possibility of generating large riches is one of the primary drivers of entrepreneurship. Entrepreneurs understand that profitable company endeavors can generate significant financial gains that might not be possible through typical employment. Entrepreneurs who can accumulate wealth benefit from increased financial security, a higher standard of life, and the capacity to pursue their professional and personal ambitions. Financial goals are closely linked to the need for freedom and control. Through entrepreneurship, one has the opportunity to control their financial future and escape the constraints of salary ceilings and corporate hierarchies. Entrepreneurs enjoy having control over financial choices, including how to allocate revenues and develop investment strategies as well as how to grow and reinvest in the company.

Taking calculated risks to achieve financial goals implies possible benefits. Entrepreneurs are aware of the risks and difficulties associated with starting a firm, but they are prepared to overcome them to be financially successful. Entrepreneurs take calculated risks because they have the potential for significant returns on investment and enjoy the thrill of converting an original idea into a successful business. Entrepreneurs frequently see their projects as ways to build riches for future generations and leave a lasting legacy. A successful firm might offer the opportunity for the entrepreneur's family to experience long-term financial success. Future generations will feel the tangible effects of generational wealth creation, which will give them a solid basis on which to build their aspirations.

Entrepreneurs can invest in their goals and realize creative concepts by having financial objectives. Research, development, and the hunt for ground-breaking ideas can all be funded by money made from business ventures. Entrepreneurs understand that achieving financial success gives them the means to support their innovative ideas and promote growth in their respective industries. Entrepreneurs with financial goals are frequently aware of the chance to improve their communities.

Successful enterprises can reinvest their profits in the community, which fosters philanthropic activities, economic development, and the creation of jobs. Entrepreneurs see monetary success as a way to help and better the communities where they live.

To feel free and flexible in their life, entrepreneurs pursue financial success. A comfortable lifestyle, the freedom to pursue hobbies and interests, and the ability to take advantage of new chances are all directly related to financial success. Business success allows people to enjoy their lives without being constrained by money.

People's dreams for financial success are a major factor in what motivates them to become entrepreneurs. Entrepreneurs are driven to confront the difficulties and uncertainties of business ownership by the appeal of wealth creation as well as the possibility of independence, legacy-building, and impact. These ambitions support not only the individual entrepreneur's journey but also economic expansion, inventiveness, and the general advancement of industries.

3. Creativity and innovation

Entrepreneurs frequently have a burning ambition to invent and produce something new. It can be exciting to think about introducing novel concepts, goods, or services to the market. The joy of turning abstract ideas into concrete realities that might fill wants or reshape industries is what feeds the entrepreneurial spirit. Entrepreneurship thrives on innovation and creativity because they provide the journey vitality, originality, and the opportunity for profound change. These two factors provide entrepreneurs the ability to question norms, come up with fresh ideas, and rethink entire sectors. Let's explore further how entrepreneurship is fueled by innovation and creativity.

Innovation is the process of introducing novel concepts, practices, goods, or services that result in substantial change. It entails thinking outside the box and developing solutions that satisfy unmet requirements or enhance current procedures. On the other side, creativity entails coming up with original ideas, concepts, and viewpoints that spur innovation. Entrepreneurship requires both innovation and creativity, which work together to advance society.

Complex problem identification and resolution are what entrepreneurs excel at. They can tackle problems from novel perspectives thanks to their creativity and innovation, which produces ground-breaking solutions. Entrepreneurs use their innovative thinking to tackle complicated problems head-on, whether it's creating new technology to simplify operations or producing a product that fulfills a particular niche demand.

Disruptive concepts that go against accepted conventions and sectors are a common form of innovation. Entrepreneurs have the power to restructure entire industries when they propose disruptive innovations, which are those that transform marketplaces and redefine how things are done. Consider how businesses like Uber, Airbnb, and Netflix upended established business structures and revolutionized their respective industries. Entrepreneurs can adjust to shifting market conditions thanks to their creativity and invention. Entrepreneurs can change their business concepts, goods, or services to stay current by paying attention to consumer demands and market developments. In the face of technological breakthroughs and changing consumer preferences, this capacity for evolution is essential.

Innovative entrepreneurial endeavors foster a culture that values and promotes original thought.

This entails creating an atmosphere where staff members feel free to contribute ideas, try new things, and take measured risks. Such a culture can provide a consistent flow of original ideas and a vibrant, forward-thinking company. Entrepreneurs frequently iterate through the innovation process, honing and improving their concepts over time. This iterative cycle is fueled by creativity, which enables business owners to discover opportunities in setbacks, learn from mistakes, and pivot toward better solutions. For sustainable growth, this ongoing improvement is crucial.

User-centric design thinking typically forms the core of innovation. Entrepreneurs have empathy for their target market and are aware of their needs and wants. This comprehensive knowledge directs the development of goods and services that cater to client demands, encouraging loyalty and standing out in crowded markets. Entrepreneurs who are innovative and creative can have a huge impact on society and the economy. They bring about new goods and services that improve people's lives as well as jobs and economic progress. Technology, sustainability, and other fields like healthcare and education may all benefit society in significant ways.

Collaboration and a range of viewpoints:
Environments that value collaboration and a diversity of viewpoints foster innovation. Interdisciplinary teams with members from several fields are frequently sought after by entrepreneurs. This diversity encourages the exchange of ideas and spawns original thoughts that might not have developed otherwise.

The vision that entrepreneurs have for their businesses is fueled by creativity. It gives them the ability to look beyond their current problems and picture a time when their discoveries will have a lasting effect. This forward-looking mindset encourages tenacity, fortitude, and the pursuit of excellence.

Entrepreneurship is centered on innovation and creativity, which inspire people to venture into new territory and push the limits of what is possible. These factors give entrepreneurs the ability to develop innovative solutions, adapt to shifting conditions, and promote societal and economic advancement. Entrepreneurs impact not just their fates but also the development of industries and the trajectory of human progress by fusing creative thinking and innovative action.

4. Passion and Purpose

Many business owners are motivated by their interests and a desire to integrate their work with their underlying principles and values. Businesses that are based on causes, passions, or missions have the potential to have a significant positive impact on society and serve a greater purpose.

In the heart of entrepreneurship, passion, and purpose are twin flames that burn brilliantly, giving the journey purpose, dedication, and a profound sense of fulfillment. Entrepreneurs who pursue their businesses with sincere enthusiasm and a sense of greater purpose frequently discover themselves on a transforming journey that goes beyond financial success. Let's explore how entrepreneurship is fueled by passion and purpose:

The extreme, emotionally driven enthusiasm for anything is referred to as passion. People are motivated to devote their time, effort, and resources to a particular project by a deep-seated emotion. On the other hand, purpose extends beyond individual excitement. In line with one's basic values and beliefs, purpose and awareness sense that one's actions have a significant impact on the world.

Entrepreneurs who pursue businesses that are motivated by passion and purpose frequently discover that they are expressing their true selves. Customers and business partners respond favorably to this sincerity, forging bonds that go beyond simple business dealings. This congruence with sincerity promotes strong bonds and trust.

Entrepreneurs have the resiliency and determination required to overcome obstacles because of their passion and purpose. Entrepreneurs are enabled to continue pushing forward by their intrinsic motivation, which comes from a sincere enthusiasm for the business and a sense of purpose. Their unrelenting dedication to their vision fuels their motivation. Entrepreneurs with a passion for solving problems in the real world are motivated to do so. As a result of their passion, they go above and beyond to comprehend client demands, identify pain points, and create goods or services that change the world. Because these businesspeople want to make a positive difference in society, purpose adds another dimension of significance.

Passionate and purposeful business owners frequently develop a devoted consumer base and a network of supporters. Customers are drawn to a company's goal and principles as well as its product or service. This commitment goes beyond business dealings, fostering enduring connections. A profound sense of personal fulfillment results from following your passion and purpose. Entrepreneurs like and feel satisfied when their job reflects their inner principles because they know that their efforts serve the greater good. Beyond financial success, this internal motivation propels entrepreneurs to keep going even in the face of obstacles.

Entrepreneurs who are driven by passion and purpose encourage others to do the same. They serve as lighthouses for people who want to change the world because of the sincerity of their endeavors and the impact they have. Aspiring business owners are motivated by their experiences to carve out successful careers and make significant contributions. Businesses may survive and thrive if they are driven by passion and purpose. Entrepreneurs who are emotionally invested in their businesses are more likely to value ethical behavior and have a long-term vision. They take into account how decisions will affect the environment, society, and ethics.

Businesses with a purpose-driven mission frequently serve as catalysts for larger social change. They aid in beneficial changes that go beyond their domains of influence by addressing societal issues and fighting for causes. Entrepreneurs who are passionate and driven by a cause take a human-centered approach. Empathy and a sincere wish to improve people's lives are the driving forces behind their relationships with clients, staff, and stakeholders.

Entrepreneurs are propelled on a journey of authenticity, influence, and fulfillment by a powerful mix of their passion and purpose. These motivational factors touch the very essence of human drive and potential, transcending simple financial gain. Entrepreneurs who inject passion and purpose into their businesses not only shape their destinies but also have an impact on the world at large, leaving a legacy of significant contributions and constructive change.

5. Flexible scheduling and work-life balance

For some businesspeople, living a balanced lifestyle is what motivates them. The independence that comes with owning a business opens the door to remote work opportunities, flexible work schedules, and a better separation of work and personal life.

For many businesses, flexibility and work-life balance serve as pillars of appeal, promising a dynamic and harmonious way to manage professional and personal endeavors. These factors give people the chance to break free from the rigidity of conventional work arrangements and create a lifestyle that suits their preferences and well-being. Let's delve more into the ways that adaptability and work-life balance influence the entrepreneurial landscape:

Entrepreneurial flexibility is the ability to choose one's working hours, environment, and method of operation. It enables business owners to customize their work schedules to meet their unique demands, maximizing productivity and well-being. Contrarily, work-life balance ensures that personal and professional obligations are equal and don't conflict with one another. The freedom it offers in terms of work hours is one of the most enticing features of entrepreneurship. Entrepreneurs have the freedom to choose the hours that best suit their productivity peaks, whether those be early mornings, late nights, or irregular hours. They can coordinate their job with their circadian rhythms and increase productivity thanks to their autonomy.

Entrepreneurial flexibility frequently includes the freedom to conduct business from any location. With the help of modern technology, business owners may operate remotely, dissolving distance constraints and enabling a mobile lifestyle. A sense of emancipation is cultivated by having the option to choose one's workplace, whether it be a home office or a café by the beach. Entrepreneurs are free to create the organizational structures that suit their interests. This can entail putting novel strategies into practice, like the "4-day workweek" or adopting project-based timetables. Entrepreneurs design their work environments outside of the confines of conventional 9-to-5 norms to maximize productivity, creativity, and well-being.

The goal of work-life balance is to seamlessly combine personal and professional obligations. Entrepreneurs don't have to sacrifice their business objectives to take care of their families, hobbies, or self-care. This integration promotes overall well-being and averts role compartmentalization related burnout. Entrepreneurs can avoid the burden of commuting by working remotely or by keeping flexible hours. This time-saving feature aids in lowering stress levels, boosting productivity, and improving quality of life.

The time wastage that might happen in typical work situations is minimized by flexible work arrangements. Entrepreneurs can concentrate on things that are of the utmost importance, streamline their processes, and steer clear of meetings or other distractions that are frequent in traditional office settings. Entrepreneurs may give their health and well-being priority by achieving a work-life balance. Without feeling limited by set timetables, they can set aside time for self-care activities like exercise and relaxation. This individualized strategy for well-being promotes both good physical and emotional health.

Entrepreneurs who value work-life balance frequently improve their interpersonal connections. Spending time with loved ones in a meaningful way strengthens bonds and promotes a sense of belonging. Entrepreneurs can communicate in meaningful ways that improve their emotional health. A crucial element in avoiding burnout is the ability to establish limits and keep a healthy work-life balance. Entrepreneurs can prevent the tiredness that comes from excessive labor and ongoing stress by actively prioritizing their health.

Flexibility and work-life balance are essential components of entrepreneurship that let people design lifestyles that are in line with their priorities and values. These components encourage productivity, creativity, and well-being in entrepreneurs by enabling them to thrive in a way that goes beyond conventional organizational structures. Entrepreneurs can start on a meaningful journey that embraces the whole gamut of human experiences by achieving a harmonic balance between their personal and professional lives.

6. Impact and Legacy

One of the goals of entrepreneurs is to leave a lasting legacy. For people who want to leave their imprint on the world, the possibility of creating a company that can survive decades and have a lasting impact on communities and sectors is a major motivator. Entrepreneurs are profoundly motivated by legacy and impact, which inspires them to launch businesses that go beyond short-term success and have a lasting impact on society. While impact demonstrates the ambition to make positive change that has an impact on society, the pursuit of legacy is a testament to the desire to create something that endures beyond the entrepreneur's lifetime. Let's delve more into how legacy and effect motivate entrepreneurship:

An entrepreneur's legacy is the ongoing influence and contributions they leave behind. It is the physical representation of the entrepreneur's goals, ideals, and achievements that will continue to have an impact on future generations. The tangible and advantageous impacts that an entrepreneur's activities, goods, or services have on society, markets, or communities are referred to as impact.

Entrepreneurs who aim to leave a legacy and make an impact want to effect long-lasting change. Their endeavors aim to change entire industries, societal conventions, or even the way individuals live and work, going beyond fads or short-term advantages. These businesspeople are aware of their ability to make a significant impact on the world. Entrepreneurs that are driven by legacy have a long-term vision that directs their efforts. They are prepared to put time, energy, and money into projects that might not provide benefits right away. They distinguish themselves from short-term thinkers by being prepared to postpone pleasure in favor of the greater good.

Entrepreneurs who have an emphasis on impact look for novel ways to solve societal problems. They are aware that their goods and services have the power to change people's lives for the better, advance sustainability, boost wellbeing, or tackle urgent problems like healthcare, education, poverty, and the environment. Entrepreneurs with a strong sense of legacy motivate younger generations by demonstrating what is possible. Their successes and the values they uphold serve as examples for young businesspeople, inspiring them to set higher goals and pursue projects that benefit society.

Building generational wealth that can benefit families and communities is a common component of leaving a legacy. Entrepreneurs who place a strong emphasis on leaving a lasting legacy build enterprises that can offer employment possibilities to their offspring, ensuring future generations' financial stability and success. Cultural changes are influenced by entrepreneurs who want to have an impact on ten. They question accepted conventions and shape public opinion, bringing about reforms that support inclusion, diversity, moral business conduct, and social responsibility.

Philanthropic initiatives are frequently incorporated into the ventures of legacy-driven entrepreneurs. They are aware that achieving success entails a duty to give back to society. These businesspeople support social issues, give to charitable organizations, and engage in philanthropy. Entrepreneurs who place a premium on legacy and effect assess success in terms other than financial measures. They consider their initiatives' impacts on people's lives, communities, and the wider world in addition to their profits. They are motivated to make choices that are consistent with their values by this complete approach to success.

Entrepreneurs who place a premium on impact and legacy work to empower people and communities. Their inventions frequently offer individuals the means, resources, and chances they need to realize their potential, face obstacles head-on, and live better lives.

Entrepreneurs are driven by legacy and impact as they travel on a transformative path. Entrepreneurs contribute to the advancement of markets, society, and people by pursuing projects that leave a legacy and effect constructive change. These businesspeople become architects of transformation via their vision, tenacity, and dedication to changing the world, leaving behind legacies that motivate and uplift future generations.

7. Getting Around Market Gaps

Finding market inefficiencies or unmet requirements is the driving force behind many entrepreneurial endeavors. Entrepreneurs are adept at spotting gaps in existing solutions and working to fill those gaps through the provision of goods or services that are tailored to particular needs. Identifying unmet needs and developing creative solutions is a strategic goal that encourages entrepreneurship. Entrepreneurs who flourish in this field have a sharp eye for detail, a thorough grasp of consumer psychology, and the capacity to develop goods or services that fill current gaps in the market. Let's explore in greater detail how entrepreneurs bridge market gaps and build worthwhile businesses:

Entrepreneurs who are competent at negotiating market gaps are also skilled at spotting unmet needs in particular markets or communities. They track patterns, pay attention to consumer feedback, and carry out in-depth studies to find gaps in the performance of current solutions. They can spot possible disruptive chances thanks to their deep insight. Successful businesspeople understand the problems, disappointments, and aspirations of their target market. These businesspeople may create solutions that specifically address the problems people have by developing a thorough awareness of client needs.

To navigate market gaps, an entrepreneur must provide unique solutions that set their business distinct from rivals. Whether it's through innovation, increased functionality, or enhanced user experiences, entrepreneurs concentrate on developing goods or services that offer distinctive value propositions. Entrepreneurs who are skilled at navigating market gaps tailor their services to precisely meet the demands observed. They make sure that clients get the most out of their goods or services by customizing their solutions to target certain pain spots.

Entrepreneurs must be quick and flexible to navigate market gaps. In response to shifting market dynamics and shifting consumer tastes, they must be prepared to reassess their strategy and products. Their solutions' adaptability guarantees that they will be useful in the future. Entrepreneurs with a keen sense of market opportunity frequently create new markets or sectors. By addressing unmet or underserved requirements, they propose solutions that open up completely new markets. This attitude of innovation has the potential to have a big impact on the market.

Market-savvy businesspeople remain on top of trends and foresee changes in consumer behavior. These businesspeople may position themselves to seize new possibilities by keeping up with rising technologies, shifting demographics, and growing consumer tastes. Entrepreneurs use a test-and-iterate strategy to bridge gaps in the market. They create minimum viable products (MVPs) to test their hypotheses and receive input from early adopters about the goods in real-world settings. They can improve their solutions and guarantee that they are in line with customer needs thanks to this iterative approach.

Successfully navigating market gaps can result in scalable businesses that expand quickly. Entrepreneurs with the ability to spot and fill important gaps have the opportunity to reach new markets and draw in a large consumer base.
Market-savvy businesspeople can spur an industry's progress. They challenge accepted practices, upend conventional business models, and encourage other industry participants to innovate by presenting cutting-edge solutions.

The dynamic process of navigating market gaps promotes entrepreneurship. Successful businesspeople launch projects that fill unmet needs, handle urgent issues, and open up new horizons. These entrepreneurs contribute to the evolution of the sector and make significant contributions that are seen by customers and communities by comprehending client pain areas, creating unique solutions, and embracing agility.

8. overcoming Challenges

The path of entrepreneurship is paved with difficulties and unknowns. Some people find inspiration in taking on these difficulties head-on, pushing their limits, and demonstrating their fortitude in the face of difficulty. The journey of the entrepreneur includes overcoming obstacles, which calls for tenacity, adaptability, and a growth mentality. Entrepreneurs must overcome a variety of challenges, from financial limitations to market uncertainties, that put their tenacity and innovation to the test. The course of an entrepreneur's business is frequently determined by how well they manage and overcome these obstacles. Let's explore the art of entrepreneurial challenge resolution in more detail:

Entrepreneurship will inevitably involve difficulties, and overcoming them requires resilience. Resilient entrepreneurs see obstacles as passing phases and seize the chance to improve. They overcome setbacks with renewed vigor and a dedication to doing better. Entrepreneurs who succeed in overcoming obstacles exhibit a growth attitude. They view difficulties as chances for growth on the personal and professional fronts. Instead of avoiding challenges, they welcome them as opportunities to pick up new knowledge, develop fresh perspectives, and advance personally.

Problem-solving and creativity are sparked by challenges. Entrepreneurs frequently explore alternative approaches that others might not have thought of to develop creative answers to challenging issues. The act of overcoming obstacles develops a proactive and resourceful mindset. Entrepreneurs who successfully navigate obstacles are also proficient at changing with the times. They are aware of the ongoing changes in markets, technologies, and consumer preferences. They adapt their techniques to fit the situation by remaining flexible and adaptable.

Setbacks are viewed by entrepreneurs as stepping stones to success. An obstacle that seems insurmountable can become a chance for development, education, and transformation. Entrepreneurs make use of losses to reevaluate their strategies, hone their products, and grow stronger. Although setbacks are a natural part of the entrepreneurial path, successful businesspeople learn from their mistakes. They examine the variables that contributed to failure, glean important knowledge, and apply this understanding to steer clear of repeating the same errors in the future.

Entrepreneurship is inherently uncertain, and addressing ambiguity is necessary to overcome obstacles. Entrepreneurs who succeed in an uncertain environment stay adaptable, change course when necessary, and make wise choices based on the knowledge at hand. Entrepreneurs who seek advice and mentoring succeed in overcoming obstacles. They understand the importance of taking advice from people who have already overcome comparable challenges. Mentorship offers a network of allies, guidance, and viewpoints that can help overcome challenges.

Financial, human, or temporal restrictions are frequent components of challenges. Entrepreneurs who are successful in overcoming obstacles carefully utilize their resources, taking calculated actions to maximize their influence and accomplish their objectives. It's important to acknowledge and appreciate even the tiniest victories when overcoming obstacles. Entrepreneurs are more driven to strive toward longer-term objectives when they receive acknowledgment of their accomplishments, no matter how small.

It takes a special kind of perseverance, ingenuity, adaptability, and growth mentality to overcome obstacles. Successful businesspeople see obstacles as chances for progress, creativity, and self-improvement. Entrepreneurs who overcome obstacles with tenacity not only influence the course of their businesses but also show that they can succeed in the always-changing environment of entrepreneurship.

9. Desire for Growth

Entrepreneurs frequently look for professional and personal growth opportunities that regular employment may not provide. The entrepreneurial journey is a lifelong learning process that encompasses gaining new knowledge, broadening one's perspectives, and developing personally. Entrepreneurs are driven to push the envelope, build their businesses, and reach new heights of success by their innate passion for growth. This motivation stems from the desire to advance both personally and professionally and from the desire to have a long-lasting influence on markets and industries. Let's explore how entrepreneurship is shaped by the need for growth:

An appetite for learning and skill improvement is fueled by the drive for progress. Entrepreneurs understand that in the constantly changing business environment, remaining stationary is not an option. They look for chances to learn, whether through formal education, independent study, or working with subject-matter experts. Entrepreneurs who want to expand view change as a chance rather than a problem. To remain relevant in cutthroat markets, they are prepared to adjust their methods, adopt new technologies, and investigate cutting-edge ideas. They can handle changes in customer behavior and business trends because of their agility.

Scaling business initiatives and operations is a crucial component of growth. Entrepreneurs who have a growth mindset picture their businesses expanding into new markets, reaching larger audiences, and becoming more profitable. They create plans to expand distribution, market reach, and manufacturing. Entrepreneurs who are motivated by a goal for expansion frequently venture outside of their comfort zones. They might try out new industries, test out various company ideas, or broaden their selection of goods and services. Their entrepreneurial experience remains fascinating and dynamic as a result of this exploration.

Innovation is encouraged by a drive for expansion. Entrepreneurs who are looking to expand are more inclined to invest in R&D, looking into ways to improve their offerings and remain competitive. Their businesses and the industries they work in profit from this innovation. Entrepreneurs who want to expand are aware of how crucial it is to develop a competitive advantage. They make investments in establishing powerful brands, providing outstanding customer experiences, and setting themselves apart from other businesses. This dedication to excellence increases market share and consumer loyalty.

Ten of the most successful businesspeople are those who prioritize growth. As their businesses grow, they create jobs, provide mentoring and aid in the expansion of the economy. its quest for expansion is motivated by the desire to have a beneficial effect on the lives of its partners, employees, and the general public. Resilience in the face of difficulties is stimulated by the desire for growth. Obstacles are not seen by entrepreneurs as insurmountable hurdles, but rather as stepping stones to success. Their dedication to hitting growth milestones serves as the foundation for their resolve to overcome obstacles.

Entrepreneurs who are motivated by growth establish challenging objectives and create tactical approaches to accomplish them. These objectives act as road maps, offering guidance and a feeling of direction. A sense of success and drive are increased via the process of working toward and achieving these goals. Entrepreneurs who want expansion frequently influence the development of their industries. They question norms, encourage rivals to innovate, and contribute to the general growth of their sectors by launching cutting-edge goods, services, or business strategies.

Entrepreneurs are motivated to broaden their views, innovate, and make a significant contribution by a drive for growth. This drive encourages lifelong learning, flexibility, and a dedication to excellence. Entrepreneurs who embrace growth contribute to the expansion of sectors, economies, and the entire entrepreneurial ecosystem in addition to the success of their businesses.

Motivations in the always-changing world of business are as varied as the businesses themselves. Although achieving financial success is a common goal, people start businesses for a variety of reasons that are deeply entrenched in their own goals, societal circumstances, and the search for purpose. The intricate mosaic of goals, desires, and aspirations that shape not just the entrepreneurs themselves but also the global economic fabric are revealed when we peel back the layers of entrepreneurial reasons.

Chapter 3

Building a solid financial foundation

Building a solid financial foundation depends on how you make and spend your money

how much do you earn a day, per week, a month, what are your expenses

what are your savings plans, are you into dept how bad is it, are you Inverting?

this chapter talks about how to build a solid financial foundation.

Chapter Three

Building a solid financial foundation

We now turn our attention to a few crucial pillars of financial health as we continue our investigation into financial fitness and the delicate balance between wealth and well-being: prudent debt management, retirement savings, investing wisely, diversifying your investments, and understanding risk tolerance.

1. Effective Debt Management

Debt may have two sides to it. When utilized sensibly, it can help people achieve important life goals like home ownership or education. Unmanaged or high-interest debt, however, can pose a serious threat to your financial stability. Let's look at some excellent debt management strategies.

You can start by listing all of your unpaid debts, including credit card balances, mortgages, vehicle loans, personal loans, and student loans. Debt with high interest rates should be paid off first, for instance, the interest on credit card debt can add up quickly and harm your capacity to manage your money. Create a well-organized plan for paying off your debts. The debt snowball approach (paying off the smallest debts first) and the debt avalanche method (paying off the debts with the highest interest rates first) are two popular methods.

Consider options like transferring the balance to a credit card with a lower rate or consolidating student loans with the purpose of converting high-interest debt into loans with reduced interest rates. Make sure that paying off your debt remains a top financial priority by allocating a portion of your budget to this purpose. Avoid taking on additional debt while you're trying to pay off your current debt unless it's for necessary and budgeted spending.

Effective debt management is a critical first step toward financial freedom since it frees up funds for future savings and investments.

2. Investing for the future

Building a nest egg is necessary to secure financial security in your older age, even though retirement may seem like a long way off. It can be challenging to get started, but you must do it. So take full use of any retirement benefits your employer may be providing, such as a 401(k) or 403(b). If your employer offers a match, make sure to take advantage of it because it's practically free money. If your business doesn't offer a retirement plan or if you want to increase your workplace savings, think about starting an Individual Retirement Account (IRA). Traditional IRAs (with tax-deferred contributions) and Roth IRAs (with tax-free withdrawals in retirement) are the two main forms. Depending on your preferred lifestyle, calculate how much you'll need in retirement. Calculators for retirement can help you determine your financial goal.

Contribute on a regular basis to your retirement funds, ideally by automating these payments. Your retirement funds may be significantly impacted by consistency over time. To limit risk and maximize returns, invest your retirement funds prudently by diversifying across asset types. Review your retirement savings strategy on a regular basis and make necessary adjustments. Course changes may be necessary due to factors such as shifting income, expenses, and investment performance.

Keep in mind that saving for retirement is a long-term project and that beginning early can significantly increase your financial stability. Building a strong financial base entails prioritizing retirement savings and managing debt properly, putting you on the path to obtaining both health and wealth in your later years.

We will discuss risk management techniques, as well as measures designed specifically for small business owners looking to ensure their financial future, in the pages that follow.

Without a full understanding of the essential elements of investing properly, diversifying investments, and recognizing your risk tolerance, our road toward financial health and the harmonic balance of wealth and well-being would fall short.

3. Prudent Investment

A strong financial foundation is a result of judicious investing. It is the means via which your money may increase over time. But investing is not a one-size-fits-all activity; it takes a thoughtful assessment of your financial objectives, risk tolerance, and time horizon.

Your financial objectives should be in line with your investment strategy. Long-term goals can accept higher-risk, perhaps higher-reward investments while short-term goals may call for more cautious investments. Recognize the connection between risk and profit. Riskier investments often offer a larger probability of loss along with the potential for higher profits. The profits from conservative investments may be lower, but they are less dangerous. To spread risk, diversify your financial portfolio. Keep your diversification in mind. A diverse portfolio has a variety of asset classes, including stocks, bonds, real estate, and possibly unconventional investments like commodities. Examine several investing options, such as specific equities, mutual funds, exchange-traded funds (ETFs), bonds, and real estate. Your decision should be in line with your objectives and level of risk tolerance because each has advantages and cons.

Investing is not a sprint, but a marathon. Avoid chasing after short-term gains or getting upset in response to market changes. Market turbulence can be managed with a long-term view.

4. Investment Diversification

The key to managing risk in your investment portfolio is diversification. It entails distributing your investments across a range of businesses, geographies, and asset types.

Based on your risk tolerance and time horizon, distribute your assets among several asset types, such as equities, bonds, and cash equivalents. Increase your diversification by investing in a range of sectors and industries within each asset class. As a result, a slump in any one area has less of an impact. To lessen the danger brought on by the economic realities of a particular nation, think about investing in global markets. Maintain your target asset allocation by reviewing and rebalancing your portfolio on a regular basis. Your allocation may change if some investments succeed or underperform over time.

5. Knowledge of Risk Tolerance

Prioritizing your risk tolerance while choosing an investment strategy is essential. Your capacity and willingness to put up with changes in the value of your investments are referred to as your risk tolerance. It is a very individualized component of investing and can differ greatly from person to person.

Consider your financial status, investing objectives, and attitude toward risk. Are you willing to accept the possibility of losing some of your money in exchange for a chance at larger returns? Take into account your investing horizon. A higher risk tolerance is usually possible with longer time horizons because you have more time to recover from market downturns. To help you determine your risk tolerance, many financial institutions offer risk tolerance surveys. These evaluations might help you understand how comfortable you are with different levels of risk.

Consider speaking with a financial advisor who can offer advice catered to your particular situation if you're uncertain about your risk tolerance or how to match it with your investing strategy.

You may create a solid financial foundation that supports your goals for both health and money by making prudent investments, diversifying your holdings, and matching your decisions to your risk tolerance. In future chapters, we will look into the particular financial considerations for small business owners as well as more sophisticated investing methods.

Chapter 4

What is the connection between financial health and physical health

How does your daily activity in your work place affect you when you're backe at home, do you get exhausted, tired and week?

Chapter four

The Relationship between Financial health and Physical Well-Being

It's crucial to understand the close relationship between financial health and physical health if one is to achieve financial success and a harmonic balance between wealth and well-being. This chapter explores the complex interrelationship between these two elements of our lives, highlighting the negative effects of financial stress on physical health and offering methods for easing it.

1. The impact of Financial stress on physical health

Financial stress, which is frequently brought on by debt, unemployment, or insufficient resources, can have a serious negative impact on your physical health. Financial stress can cause physical symptoms because of the strong mind-body link. When financial stress affects your mentality, it can also affect your physical health. Your physical health can be impacted by financial stress in a variety of ways.

Long-term financial stress can increase the risk of developing chronic illnesses including diabetes, high blood pressure, and heart disease. These conditions may be exacerbated by the constant stress on your body's systems. Anxiety and depression are intimately related to financial stress, and both of these mental health conditions can cause physical symptoms including exhaustion, changes in appetite, and sleep difficulties. Your immune system is weakened by ongoing stress, making you more prone to diseases and infections. This may lead to more illnesses occurring more frequently and slower healing. Insomnia and other sleep disorders are frequently brought on by financial concerns. Sleeping well is crucial for both physical and mental health.

People who are experiencing financial stress may use unhealthy coping strategies, such as binge eating, smoking, or drinking too much alcohol, which can worsen their physical health. Your capacity to enjoy daily activities and retain a positive outlook might be greatly lowered by the constant concern and strain of financial stress.

It is important to prioritize both your financial and physical well-being since you should be aware of the negative effects that financial stress can have on your health.

2. Techniques for Decreased Financial Stress

Although financial stress can be debilitating, there are doable steps you can take to lessen its effects and enhance your financial and physical health:

Create a thorough financial plan that addresses budgeting, debt management, and savings objectives. A sense of control and direction can be offered by having a roadmap.

Consult a financial advisor or counselor who can offer professional advice and help if your financial situation is exceptionally complicated or overwhelming. Peace of mind can be attained by creating and keeping an emergency fund. Anxiety about unforeseen costs might be lessened by having financial security. Create a well-thought-out strategy for debt repayment. Putting high-interest debts first, haggling with creditors, or consolidating loans are a few examples of how to do this.

Be sure to include stress-reduction strategies in your everyday routine. Exercise, mindfulness exercises, yoga, and meditation can all reduce stress and enhance both physical and mental health. Don't be afraid to ask friends and relatives for emotional assistance. Financial stress can be emotionally taxing, but it can also be relieved by talking about your worries and getting assistance. Consider speaking with a mental health expert if your mental health is being negatively impacted by financial stress. Tools for handling stress and anxiety can be found in counseling or therapy. Review your financial objectives frequently, and make any adjustments. Instead of comparing yourself to others, concentrate on your own financial journey.

A critical first step in achieving balance and well-being in both aspects of our lives is to recognize the link between physical and financial health. You may develop a happier, more prosperous future that includes both wealth and well-being by taking proactive measures to lessen financial stress and promote self-care.

We now shift our focus to three crucial areas in our investigation of the deep relationship between financial health and physical health: the significance of mental health, the crucial role of exercise, and diet in promoting general well-being.

3. Mental Health Is Important

A fundamental component of comprehensive well-being, mental health is entwined with both physical and financial well-being. Your mental health can be negatively impacted by financial stress, which can cause worry, sadness, and other emotional difficulties. Conversely, having poor mental health might make it more difficult for you to be physically well and make wise financial decisions. This is why mental health is significant in the context of our conversation:

Making financial decisions frequently calls for emotional stability, clarity, and attention. Making reasonable decisions about spending, saving, and investing is more difficult when your mental health is impacted. How well you deal with stress is greatly influenced by your mental health. People who are in good mental health are better able to use appropriate coping mechanisms, such as asking for help and making wise financial decisions. Motivation and goal-setting are supported by a sound mental condition. When you're psychologically healthy, you're more inclined to put your physical health over money and plan and work toward financial goals. Your resilience to financial misfortunes is increased by mental health. It gives you the psychological tools you need to overcome financial setbacks and persevere in your efforts to achieve your physical and financial objectives. The importance of mental health is highlighted by the necessity of a holistic approach to overall well-being, in which financial stability, physical fitness, and mental well-being are intertwined.

4. Incorporating exercise in Your Daily Routine

Exercise may be easily incorporated into your daily routine, even if you have a hectic financial schedule, and it is an effective strategy for promoting both physical and mental health. You need to exercise, and I'll explain why.

Regular exercise can improve cardiovascular health, immunity, and general physical fitness while lowering the risk of chronic diseases. In turn, this can lower healthcare expenses and improve your financial situation. Exercise releases endorphins, or "feel-good" hormones, which have been shown to be a natural stress reliever. Physical exercise can help lessen the effects of anxiety and sadness. You may receive the benefits without spending hours in the gym. Workouts that are brief and regular can be beneficial. Take into account exercises like brisk walking, at-home workouts, or even working out during your daily commute.

Put exercise on the same level of importance as a finance meeting or professional requirement by arranging it into your day. You are more likely to stick with it if you set out particular periods for exercise. Think about finding a workout buddy or enrolling in a fitness program or organization. You can maintain your regimen with the aid of accountability.

5. Nutrition and the Effect It Has on Your Health

Your body and mind are both powered by nutrition. It has a significant impact on your physical health, mental health, and even financial health. Your overall health is impacted by nutrition in ways such as

Essential nutrients for biological processes, such as energy production and immune system support, are provided by a balanced diet. Reduced risk of diet-related diseases and increased general vigor are benefits of good nutrition. A rising corpus of research is showing a connection between nutrition and mental health. A diet high in antioxidants, B vitamins, and omega-3 fatty acids can boost brain function and elevate mood. Eating healthfully can be affordable. Over time, there can be significant savings achieved by meal planning, cooking at home, and cutting back on eating out frequently. Consider making meal preparation a part of your routine. Making meals ahead of time can help you save time and money and guarantee that you have access to a variety of wholesome options.

By enjoying each bite and being attentive to your hunger and fullness indicators, you can practice mindful eating. This can assist in reducing overeating and fostering a healthier connection with food. Remember how important it is to drink enough water. Fatigue, emotional fluctuations, and impaired cognitive function can result from dehydration. Making healthy eating and exercise choices will improve both your physical and mental health, giving you the vigor and focus you need to make wise financial decisions.

You can create a life where all three aspects are beautifully balanced by realizing the holistic relationship between your financial health, bodily health, and mental well-being. The practical methods for setting up a healthy workspace, maximizing productivity, and making money while promoting your well-being will be covered in more detail in the next chapters.

Chapter 5
Creating a Healthy Workspace

Your workspace should not be too rigid,there should be room for stretching and taking regular breaks

Raphael was so focused on work and making more money that he forget that health also matters

We will understand the importance of creating a healthy working space, the benefits and staying productive

Chapter Five

Creating a Healthy Workspace

It's crucial to recognize the critical impact that our workplace plays on our general health and productivity as we pursue financial fitness and well-being. The design of a healthy workspace is discussed in this chapter, with a focus on the value of ergonomics and work-life balance in fostering physical and mental well-being.

1. Creating an ergonomic workplace

Your physical health and productivity are significantly influenced by the layout of your workstation. Your requirements are catered to, resulting in a work atmosphere that promotes comfort, effectiveness, and well-being. Take into account the following while planning your workspace:

Purchase a chair and workstation that encourage healthy posture. Your desk should be at a comfortable height, and your chair should offer lumbar support. To lessen pressure on your neck and eyes, place your computer monitor at eye level. If necessary, use a monitor stand that is adjustable. To avoid wrist strain, choose an ergonomic keyboard and mouse. Use a wrist rest if you need further assistance.

Make sure your desk has enough light to prevent eye fatigue. The best lighting is natural light, but if that's not possible, utilize strategically placed artificial lighting. To avoid trip risks and preserve a clutter-free environment, tidy cables and cords. Use a footrest to maintain a healthy posture if your feet cannot rest comfortably on the floor. Include frequent pauses and exercise in your workday. To counteract the harmful effects of extended sitting, stretch, move around, and switch positions.

Decorate your workstation with things that uplift and encourage you. Your general well-being can be improved by including plants, artwork, or inspirational phrases. Having an ergonomic workstation is essential for avoiding physical pain, stress, and injuries that can have an adverse effect on your general health and work productivity.

2. Techniques for Preventing Burnout

Burnout is a condition brought on by ongoing working stress that involves both physical and emotional exhaustion. It is crucial to recognize and put prevention measures in place since it can have serious effects on your physical and mental health. Avoid burnout by taking these simple actions.

Set realistic deadlines and order things according to importance to avoid feeling overloaded. Stress can be decreased and productivity can be increased with good time management. Set definite, attainable objectives for your job tasks. Constant tension and disappointment might result from having unrealistic expectations. Limit your commitment. When you're already managing a significant workload, choose your projects and activities carefully. Say no more often.

When appropriate, assign duties to others if you have the capacity to do so. By delegating, you not only lighten your load but also give others a chance to develop. Taking breaks frequently can help prevent burnout. Your mind can be refreshed by taking brief breaks from your work, stretching out quickly, or taking a short walk. Your work hours should be precisely stated and adhered to. Outside of these hours, resist the need to constantly check for work-related texts.

Include stress-reduction strategies into your everyday routine, such as mindfulness exercises, deep breathing exercises, and meditation. If you're feeling overwhelmed, don't be afraid to ask your employer or coworkers for help. Fair accommodations and support can result from open dialogue.

3. The Advantages of Consistent Breaks

Regular breaks aren't just a luxury; they're essential for preserving your well-being and productivity throughout the course of the working day. The following are just a few of the many advantages of including breaks in your workday:

When you return to your work activities after a break, your focus and productivity may increase. The chance to step away from pressures, unwind, and recharge is provided by brief breaks. This can improve brain clarity and lower overall stress levels. By giving your mind time to wander and form new connections, breaks can boost creativity. Breaks give you a chance to get up and move about, stretch, and ease any pain from prolonged sitting or repetitive motions.

Regular breaks help lessen the stress, exhaustion, and burnout that come with working nonstop. By allowing time for reflection, taking pauses can help you make decisions that are well-thought-out and well-informed. Breaks help you maintain a healthier work-life balance by allowing you to schedule time for personal duties and self-care. We'll cover work-life balance in more detail in the chapter after this one.

By lowering the hazards connected to sedentary behavior and encouraging stress management, regular breaks can improve long-term physical health.

Strategic and thoughtful break-taking is essential if you want to experience these advantages. A 5- to 10-minute break per hour can be quite useful in preserving your physical and mental health and improving overall work effectiveness.

Chapter 6
Work life balance

How do you balance your work and your life, do you work get back home sleep wake up the next da, back to work and so on
Raphael did the same thing. He only concentrated on making money and forgot that health is welth. relationship is also wealth

this chapter talks about balancing work live and outside work live as well

Chapter Six

Work-life balance

Maintaining Harmony in Entrepreneurship through Work-Life Balance

The harmony between the demands of work and personal responsibilities is known as work-life balance. Due to the frequently demanding and unpredictable nature of starting and operating a business, finding a work-life balance may be particularly difficult for entrepreneurs. To preserve one's physical and mental health, to be productive, and to avoid burnout, one must find a balance. Here's a closer look at how entrepreneurs might combine work and family.

1. Important Components of Work-Life Balance:

1. Work-life balance requires setting aside time for both professional obligations and private pursuits like family, hobbies, exercise, and leisure. Time allocation is the deliberate division of your free time among various obligations. It entails setting priorities for tasks based on their significance, urgency, and alignment with your objectives. Effective time management is a crucial ability for entrepreneurs since it has a direct impact on their

level of productivity, work-life balance, and business performance as a whole.

2. Establishing distinct lines of demarcation between work and personal life is crucial. To prevent work from consuming personal time, entrepreneurs require set working hours. The boundaries you set to define your personal and professional space, time, energy, and interactions are referred to as boundaries in the context of entrepreneurship. These boundaries assist you in managing expectations, achieving a healthy and long-lasting work-life balance, and preserving your physical and emotional well-being. Entrepreneurs who successfully establish and uphold boundaries are better able to manage their obligations, avoid burnout, and cultivate fruitful connections. and pay attention.

3. Prioritization: Making a list of priorities_ is essential. Business owners should concentrate on things that directly advance their companies and their own well-being. Determining the relative priority and urgency of tasks, activities, and goals is the process of prioritization. Effective prioritization is crucial for managing time, resources, and energy in the hectic world of entrepreneurship. Entrepreneurs with strong prioritization skills may concentrate on high-impact tasks, make wise choices, and accomplish their goals quickly.

4. Delegating and outsourcing: Entrepreneurs can maintain balance by contracting out non-core operations or outsourcing work that can be done by others. Entrepreneurs can effectively use their resources, time, and skills by delegating and outsourcing some tasks. Trying to oversee every element of your firm as an entrepreneur might result in burnout and slow growth. While outsourcing entails hiring outside help to carry out particular duties, delegation entails assigning responsibilities within your organization. Both techniques let business owners concentrate on things that have a big impact, boost productivity, and expand their companies. Here is a thorough examination of outsourcing and delegation:

Delegation.

Determine which tasks team members with the requisite knowledge and experience can complete successfully. To prevent misconceptions, be sure to express the task's parameters, requirements, and objectives clearly. Give team members activities that will help them develop, so they may improve their abilities and make valuable contributions. Put your team's performance in their capable hands. Hold them responsible for the outcomes while providing the assistance and resources they need. Foster a culture of continual development by giving those you assigned duties regular feedback and encouragement.

Outsourcing.

Examine duties that are not essential, time-consuming, or call for specialist knowledge not already in-house. Pick dependable outside suppliers who meet the requirements and standards of your company. To avoid misunderstandings, create precise contracts that specify the scope, deliverables, deadlines, and expectations. Keep lines of communication open with your contracted partners to ensure alignment and to quickly handle any problems. Make sure your requirements are met by keeping an eye on the caliber of the work produced by your outsourcing partners.

5. Prioritizing self-care, such as engaging in physical activity, getting enough sleep, and engaging in mental wellness activities, improves general well-being. The deliberate practice of looking after your physical, mental, and emotional well-being is known as self-care. Self-care is crucial in the fast-paced and demanding world of entrepreneurship for preserving your health, controlling stress, and upholding your general quality of life. Self-care is important, and neglecting it can result in burnout, decreased productivity, and poor decision-making. Entrepreneurs can succeed

both personally and professionally by embracing self-care. Here's more information on the idea of self-care.

6. Flexibility: Flexibility is crucial, along with upholding boundaries. Occasionally, scheduling changes may be necessary due to business needs. Flexibility and work-life balance are closely related ideas that enhance an individual's overall effectiveness and well-being, particularly in the context of entrepreneurship. Flexibility includes the capacity to modify and adjust one's schedule, tasks, and method of working, whereas work-life balance entails achieving harmony between professional obligations and personal pursuits.

7. Entrepreneurs should withdraw from work occasionally, especially during downtime, to refuel and prevent burnout. To intentionally detach from digital gadgets, work-related activities, and online interactions in order to psychologically, emotionally, and physically recharge is known as unplugging. Unplugging has grown more crucial in today's hyperconnected society where continual communication and information intake are the norm to maintain work-life balance, avoid burnout, and promote general wellbeing.

8. Quality Time: It's crucial to prioritize quality over quantity. Relationships are improved by spending quality time together. The intentional and

concentrated interactions with family, friends, or oneself that are marked by sincere participation, emotional connection, and shared experiences are referred to as quality time. Quality time is essential for fostering relationships, lowering stress, and improving overall life satisfaction in the context of work-life balance and well-being.

2. The advantages of work-life balance for business owners.

Maintaining work-life balance helps to prevent burnout, which can have a severe influence on one's physical and emotional health. The prevention of burnout, a condition brought on by extended stress and overwork and characterized by physical, emotional, and cerebral depletion, depends heavily on work-life balance. Finding a balance between your professional obligations and personal needs as an entrepreneur is crucial for sustaining your health, productivity, and long-term success. Here are some ways that work-life balance helps to stop burnout.

Enhanced Productivity: Entrepreneurs who get better sleep, are more focused and are able to manage their time well are more productive. Work-life balance is a purposeful method that increases productivity, not only about separating work and personal life. You may promote greater productivity, focus, and general effectiveness by prioritizing time for both work-related activities and your personal well-being. Here are some specific ways that work-life balance directly improves productivity.

Health and Well-Being: Balance promotes both physical and mental health, lowering the risk of illnesses brought on by stress and problems with mental health. Maintaining a healthy work-life balance is essential for maintaining your health and general well-being. Physical vitality, mental clarity, emotional resilience, and a higher quality of life are all enhanced by striking a balance between work obligations and leisure pursuits. Here are some specific ways that work-life balance affects health and happiness:

Strengthened Relationships: Spending quality time with loved ones strengthens bonds and adds to overall satisfaction. Relationships with family, friends, and coworkers can all benefit from having a work-life balance. Making time for meaningful contacts, memorable experiences, and shared activities outside of work is important for developing stronger bonds and more satisfying relationships. Here are some specific ways that work-life balance affects developing relationships:

Balance encourages a revitalized mind, which supports creativity and innovation in business. Work-life balance fosters innovation and creativity.

Maintaining a healthy balance between work-related obligations and personal pursuits and leisure time fosters the development of original concepts, creative solutions, and innovative thinking. Here are some specific ways that work-life balance directly promotes creativity and innovation: Long-term sustainable business success is more likely for entrepreneurs who keep a healthy balance in their lives. Work-life balance is a strategic approach that supports sustainable growth in your entrepreneurial ventures; it goes beyond simply finding harmony between work obligations and personal pursuits. You provide the groundwork for steady, long-term progress by placing a high priority on well-being, upholding strong relationships, and encouraging a balanced lifestyle. Here are some specific ways that work-life balance directly supports sustained growth:

Better Decision-Making: Entrepreneurs who get enough sleep make more sensible choices. In addition to being crucial for well-being, work-life balance has a direct impact on your capacity for making decisions. Finding a healthy balance between work-related obligations and personal pursuits encourages better thinking, better judgment, and better decision-making. Here are some ways that a healthy work-life balance might improve your ability to make decisions:

Positive Company Culture: Business owners who place a high priority on work-life balance set a good example for their staff and foster a more positive workplace environment. An essential component of developing and maintaining a strong workplace culture is work-life balance. An atmosphere of trust, collaboration, and general well-being is fostered when employees are encouraged to strike a healthy balance between their work obligations and personal needs. Here are some specific ways that achieving work-life balance helps to foster a great workplace culture.

Chapter 7
Maximizing Productivity and Efficiency

How well do you manage your time
to maximize your productivity?
Do you have priorities and Goals?

Do you Delegate and Outsource or
you want to do everything you're?

How well are you taking advantage
of technology?

Chapter Seven

Maximizing output and effectiveness

One of the most important aspects of our continual path toward reaching financial fitness and overall well-being is optimizing productivity and efficiency. In order to maximize your productivity in both your professional and personal interests, this chapter examines the skill of creating priorities, defining clear goals, and managing your time successfully.

1. Techniques for Time Management

Time is a limited resource, and how you use it will have a big impact on your capacity to strike a balance between material success and general well-being. Making use of efficient time management strategies will increase your productivity and help you get the most out of each day.

You must first choose which of the day's responsibilities are most crucial and time-sensitive. Create daily to-do lists that detail your tasks and responsibilities and concentrate on completing these chores first to guarantee that important goals are achieved. To keep a clear sense of direction, prioritize your list. Allocate particular time blocks for certain task categories, such as setting aside time for meetings, focused work, and breaks. Your work should be divided into focused intervals of 25 minutes, each followed by a brief break. This approach can increase focus and productivity, help you see typical distractions, and take action to reduce them. When feasible, turn off unneeded messages, employ internet blockers, or create designated quiet periods. To automate tasks, assign them to team members or use automation tools. Your time is freed up by delegation to engage in more strategic pursuits. Assemble comparable activities into a single batch and complete them. This boosts productivity and lowers the cost of mental switching. Be realistic about how much you can get done in a day; overcommitting yourself to your schedule might cause stress and lower productivity.

2. Setting priorities and goals

It's essential to define clear priorities and set specific goals in order to achieve both financial fitness and well-being. This will not only provide you direction but also aid in keeping your attention on what is most important.

Choosing what is most important in your personal and financial life can help you think about your long-term goals, values, and what makes you happy. Setting well-defined SMART goals makes it simpler to track progress and maintain motivation.

SMART goals are specific, measurable, achievable, relevant, and time-bound. Define your financial objectives, such as retirement savings, debt repayment, or emergency fund development. Determine which objectives are the most urgent and significant, and be specific about the budget and timeframe for each. Divide more ambitious goals into more manageable steps and concentrate your efforts on those that are consistent with your existing priorities. They become easier to handle and less intimidating as a result. Review your objectives frequently, and make any necessary changes. Your goals should be adaptable because priorities and life situations might change. Even just discussing your objectives with a close friend, relative, or mentor can help you feel supported and held responsible for your development.

You may construct a roadmap that directs your activities and decisions by successfully managing your time, setting priorities, and defining realistic goals. This will enable you to maximize productivity and efficiency in both your professional and personal endeavors.

3. Delegating and Contracting Out

It is a wise move to outsource duties and delegate work in order to free up your time and resources for more important pursuits. You don't have to do everything on your own if you're an individual working toward both financial success and well-being. Here are some tips on how to efficiently delegate and outsource jobs. These tasks may include bookkeeping, social media management, data entry, administrative work, and even some personal tasks. Determine your personal talents and limitations, as well as your areas of excellence and potential need for help.

If you work alone, think about outsourcing jobs or projects to independent contractors, virtual assistants, or specialized service providers. If you operate in a professional context, assigning duties to team members or colleagues based on their strengths and expertise will foster collaboration and teamwork. Platforms like Upwork, Fiverr, and Toptal may help you find qualified professionals, and while doing so, you can make sure that the individuals you delegate or outsource to are aware of your expectations and requirements. You can also offer direction and comments to make sure the assignment is completed to your satisfaction. Trusting the people or teams you give your assignment to will enable them to take charge of it and make decisions that fall within their purview of authority.

Consider the value of your time and the potential return on investment while evaluating the cost-effectiveness of outsourcing. Use the time you save through delegation and outsourcing to concentrate on high-impact tasks that support your financial and personal goals.

You may boost your productivity and efficiency while still maintaining a healthy work-life balance by delegating and outsourcing. You can allocate your time and energy more effectively to activities that support your goals by unloading duties in a deliberate manner.

4. Taking Advantage of Technology

Technology now provides a wide range of tools and resources to improve productivity and efficiency. Using technology to your advantage can speed procedures and offer insightful information, whether in your professional or personal efforts. Our ability to successfully use technology can be quite beneficial. Organizing and prioritizing your to-do lists using task management tools and applications like Asana, Trello, or Todoist. You can remain on top of deadlines and projects using these tools. Toggl or Clockify are two-time monitoring applications you might want to use to keep track of your time usage. Repetitive jobs and processes should, whenever possible, be automated. This might highlight areas where you might be less productive and help you improve. The use of financial software like QuickBooks or Xero to streamline accounting and financial management for your business is also a great way to utilize technology. These tools can help you track income and expenses, generate financial reports, and manage payroll. Email filters, autoresponders, and marketing automation tools can save you a significant amount of time. the usage of cloud storage services like Google Drive or Dropbox for document storage and sharing, while remote work and team collaboration are made possible by applications like Google Workspace. Use data analytics tools to acquire insights into your personal or corporate finances. Tools like Microsoft Power BI or Google Analytics can give you important information for making decisions. Virtual personal assistants, such as Apple's Siri or Amazon's Alexa, can assist with information retrieval, scheduling, and reminders, freeing up brain capacity. Use strong passwords, two-factor authentication, and frequent software upgrades as cybersecurity precautions to safeguard your digital assets and personal data.

You can expedite tasks, gain access to useful data, and improve your overall productivity by using technology as an ally. Technology can multiply your efforts so you can accomplish more with less, which will help you succeed financially and personally.

The following chapters will address advanced money management techniques, healthy work-life balance solutions, and how to give nutrition and well-being a high priority in daily life. These realizations will give you even more strength to live a happy life that balances material success and all-around well-being.

Chapter 8

Financial fitness for small business owners

As you seek financial goals while managing your businesses, small business entrepreneurs encounter particular financial obstacles and opportunities. The necessity of keeping personal and corporate funds separate is highlighted in this chapter's discussion of key practices for small business owners.

Chapter Eight

Financial Fitness for Small Businesses owners

As you seek financial goals while managing your businesses, small business entrepreneurs encounter particular financial obstacles and opportunities. The necessity of keeping personal and corporate funds separate is highlighted in this chapter's discussion of key practices for small business owners. Managing Business Finances is the first component right now. A small business owner's financial objectives must start with effectively managing their company's finances. It's essential to build strong financial procedures that support the expansion and sustainability of the company.

Create a business strategy and a thorough budget that details your anticipated income and expenses. This budget will act as your company's financial roadmap, directing your spending and revenue-generating efforts. You may monitor your cash flow to make sure you have enough liquidity to pay invoices, cover operating costs, and take advantage of possibilities. Managing cash flow is essential for the stability of a business.

Investment in accounting software, such as QuickBooks, Xero, or FreshBooks, to streamline financial record-keeping, track transactions, and generate financial reports, invoice clients promptly, and follow up on past-due payments. Having separate business and personal accounts will help you maintain separate bank accounts and credit cards for your business and personal finances. Pay off high-interest debt first, bargain good terms with creditors, and look into refinancing possibilities. To lessen your tax liability, engage in proactive tax preparation. To get the most out of your tax planning, write off allowable company expenses, take advantage of tax incentives, and consult a tax expert. Utilize your financial statements, such as profit and loss statements and balance sheets, to regularly analyze them in order to get knowledge of the financial health of your company.

Additionally, keeping a separate line between your personal and corporate funds is crucial for small business owners. See Separating Personal and Corporate Funds. This division has various advantages, including maintaining the limited liability status of most business forms and protecting your personal assets in the event of business liabilities or legal challenges. Separating personal and corporate finances makes tax compliance easier. It is simpler to keep track of tax-deductible company expenses, accurately record income, and adhere to tax laws. Because separating funds gives your company a more professional appearance, you can more easily understand the financial success of your company and make educated decisions without being distracted by personal spending. It reassures customers, investors, and lenders that you run your company ethically and openly. It is simpler to maintain an audit trail when your business keeps separate financial records, which can be quite helpful in the event of a tax audit or financial dispute. Separating your personal and business finances can help you set clear financial goals for both your personal and professional lives. It can also help your firm develop a strong financial history, which can be significant when applying for funding. It makes financial planning easier and guarantees efficient resource allocation.

Thirdly, risk management and business insurance. Small business management entails inherent risks, thus it's crucial to safeguard your company against unforeseen difficulties and obligations. Securing the proper commercial insurance coverage is a crucial part of effective risk management. You should also do a complete risk assessment to find any potential risks and liabilities that are unique to your company. Take into account elements including location, industry dangers, and the characteristics of your goods or services. To choose the best insurance coverage for your company, work with an insurance expert. General liability, property insurance, professional liability (errors and omissions), and workers' compensation are examples of common business insurance coverage. Review your insurance coverage from time to time to be sure it still meets your needs as your company grows. In order to take into account changes in your operations or assets, adjust policies as necessary. Create a risk management strategy that describes how your company will respond to and mitigate different hazards. Strategies for averting mishaps and minimizing financial losses should be part of this approach. Be ready for any calamities or events that can disrupt your business. Create a business continuity plan and obtain business interruption insurance. Make sure your company complies with all applicable laws and license requirements. Non-compliance may have negative legal and financial effects.

preparing for business expansion and growth. Strategic planning is crucial for small business owners to accomplish development and expansion while keeping their financial health. Here's how to efficiently plan for business expansion. Establish clear growth objectives for your company. These objectives may include raising sales, gaining more clients, introducing new goods or services, or expanding into untapped markets. To find opportunities and gauge market demand, conduct in-depth market research. For effective growth tactics, it's essential to comprehend your target market and competition. The financial requirements for your expansion plan should be outlined in financial predictions. Budgeting for marketing, hiring, and any required infrastructure investments are all part of this. Create a marketing plan to advertise your company and bring in new clients. This could include social media campaigns, digital marketing, advertising, or other promotional efforts. To assist business expansion, take into account recruiting more employees or contractors. Make sure your team has the knowledge and experience required for growth. Investigate several sources of funding for business expansion, such as bank loans, business lines of credit, venture capital, or seeking out funding from angel or venture capitalists. Keep an eye on your advancement toward your growth objectives. Depending on the outcomes you're getting, modify your approach as necessary.

Managing Legal and Tax Considerations. Managing a small business involves several legal and tax considerations. Financial stability and business lifespan depend on maintaining compliance with tax laws and legal requirements: Engage in proactive tax planning to maximize your tax strategy. To reduce your tax bill, write off allowable company expenses, benefit from tax credits, and consult a tax expert. To guarantee correct tax reporting, keep precise financial records and paperwork. To keep track of income, expenses, and tax-related data, use accounting software. Select the appropriate business legal structure, such as a corporation, partnership, limited liability company (LLC), or sole proprietorship. There are distinct legal and tax ramifications for each structure. Carefully draft and analyze agreements and contracts. Rights, responsibilities, and obligations should be spelled out in detail in contracts with partners, clients, suppliers, and workers. Protect your intellectual property, including, when necessary, patents, copyrights, and trademarks. To protect the intellectual property of your company, consult legal professionals. Keep up with local, state, and federal regulations that are relevant to your field and area. Make sure your company complies with all applicable laws and rules.

It can be difficult to navigate tax and legal problems, so consulting with accountants, lawyers, and business experts is frequently wise.

Small business owners can preserve their financial health while setting their companies for long-term success by managing risk properly, preparing for expansion, and abiding by tax and legal obligations. We shall examine other methods for leading a balanced, prosperous, and healthy life that includes both material achievement and total well-being in the chapters to come.

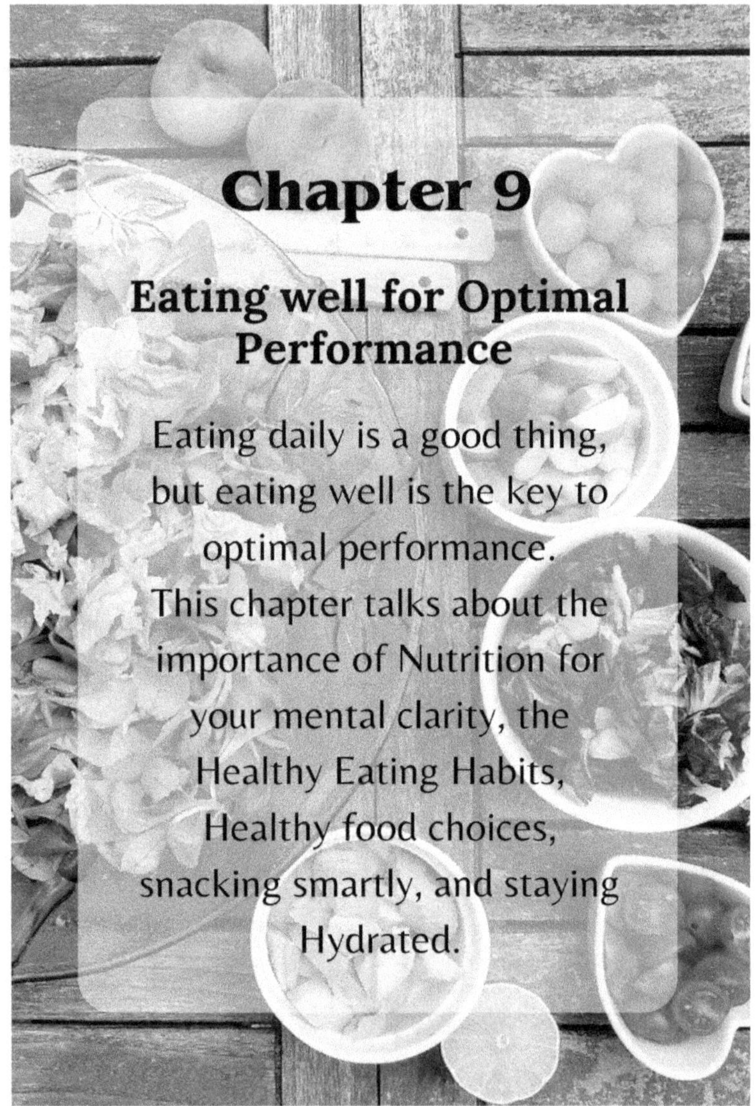

Chapter nine

Eating Well for Optimal Performance

It's crucial to understand how diet affects our brain clarity, energy levels, and general performance in our search for financial fitness and holistic well-being. This chapter discusses the significance of nutrition, along with healthy eating practices and an emphasis on nutrient-dense foods, in achieving optimum cognitive performance and physical vigor.

1. Importance of Nutrition for Energy and Mental Clarity

Our bodies and minds both need fuel, which is provided by the food we eat. The quality of our food has a major impact on how well we think, how well we can think, and how much energy we have. Our bodies are directly affected by the food we eat, how we eat, and when we eat because of this.

Omega-3 fatty acids, antioxidants, and B vitamins are vital for cognitive function, memory, and focus. The brain needs a steady supply of nutrition to perform at its optimum. Consistent energy levels are essential for prolonged work, and balanced eating helps manage blood sugar levels, minimizing energy dumps and lethargy. Complex carbohydrates and amino acids are two nutrients that have an impact on the generation of neurotransmitters that regulate mood and mental health. The ability to think creatively, make decisions, and solve problems is supported by proper nutrition.

A healthy diet can improve how well the body handles stress. Magnesium and vitamin C are nutrients that help to lessen the symptoms of stress.

2. Healthy Eating Habits

The foundation for a well-nourished body and mind is a set of healthy eating habits. Aim for a balanced diet that includes a variety of foods from all food groups, such as aiming to consume whole grains, lean proteins, healthy fats, fruits, and vegetables regularly. Also, don't forget to drink plenty of water.

Use smaller plates, measure portions, and pay attention to hunger and fullness cues to practice portion control. You should also establish a routine of regular meals and snacks throughout the day to maintain stable blood sugar levels and prevent excessive hunger. Finally, you should drink enough water each day to stay hydrated. Concentration and cognitive function might suffer from dehydration. By enjoying every bite, chewing thoroughly, and focusing on the tastes and textures of your meal, you can practice mindful eating. Trying to limit the consumption of highly processed foods, which are frequently heavy in sugar, bad fats, and additives, promotes a healthy connection with food. Choose unprocessed, whole foods. It is preferable to prepare your meals at home whenever feasible and plan them. Meal planning can help you choose healthier foods while also saving time and money. Pay attention to your body's signals of hunger and fullness, and eat only when you are truly hungry.

3. Choosing Healthy Foods

The quality of the meals you choose to eat is crucial for optimal performance, and adding nutrient-dense foods to your diet can significantly improve both your physical and mental health. The vitamins, minerals, and antioxidants found in leafy greens like spinach, kale, and Swiss chard enhance brain function.

Omega-3 fatty acids, which are crucial for brain health and mood control, are abundant in fatty fish like trout, salmon, and mackerel. With their high fiber content and long-lasting energy, whole grains like quinoa, brown rice, and oats are good for the digestive system.

Lean protein sources, such as poultry, tofu, and lentils, support muscle mass maintenance and supply the amino acids necessary for the synthesis of neurotransmitters. Antioxidants found in berries like blueberries, strawberries, and raspberries protect brain cells and enhance cognitive performance. Nuts and seeds can coexist. Healthy fats, vitamins, and minerals found in nuts and seeds like flaxseeds, almonds, and walnuts boost the health of the brain.

Bell peppers, carrots, and tomatoes are examples of colorful vegetables that are high in vitamins and antioxidants that are good for general health. Drink enough water throughout the day to maintain proper hydration, which is necessary for cognitive function.

4. Meals Planning for Busy Entrepreneurs

Setting out a certain period each week to plan your meals is quite useful; this can be a Sunday afternoon or any other convenient time in your calendar. Meal planning is an essential tool for busy entrepreneurs to ensure that they consistently consume nutritious meals despite a hectic schedule.

Planning your meals for the entire week—breakfast, lunch, supper, and snacks—will make it easier to include a range of foods and ensure a diet with a balanced intake of nutrients. Create a shopping list of the ingredients you'll need based on your meal, and stick to it when you go grocery shopping to avoid making impulse buys.

To reduce cooking time during the week, think about batch cooking or preparing ingredients in advance, such as cutting vegetables or cooking grains. Prepare portable meals or snacks, such as salads in jars, wraps, or protein-rich snacks like nuts or yogurt, that you can easily bring with you to work or meetings. When time is short, it's acceptable to rely on convenience foods like pre-cut vegetables, canned beans, or rotisserie chicken; just be sure they support your nutritional objectives. Be flexible with your meal plans because unforeseen work obligations or social engagements may need changes. When dining out, make thoughtful decisions.

5. Making Smart Snacks

Maintaining energy levels and avoiding overindulgence during meals is made possible with healthy snacking. How do you eat spherically?

Choose healthy snacks like yogurt, nuts, fresh fruit, raw vegetables, or raw vegetables. Use tiny containers or packages while snacking and be aware of portion sizes to avoid mindless munching. Avoid munching out of boredom or stress; instead, take a moment to consider how hungry you are. Choose snacks that are well-balanced and contain a mix of protein, fiber, and good fats. Examples include Greek yogurt with fruit or apple slices with almond butter. Sometimes what feels like hunger is thirst, so drink some water first to make sure you're not just dehydrated. Planned snacks should be included in your meal plan so that you always have access to healthy selections. To avoid the temptation of vending machines or unhealthy office delights, keep a supply of nutritious snacks at your place of employment.

6. Staying Hydrated

Dehydration can result in decreased concentration and weariness, making proper hydration essential for both physical and mental function. Make sure to drink water throughout the day by setting calendar or smartphone app alarms. Everywhere you go, carry a reusable water bottle with you to make it simple to consume water throughout the day. Keep track of how much water you consume each day, especially if you tend to forget to drink enough. Aim for at least eight glasses (or roughly 2 liters) each day. By infusing your water with citrus, berry, or cucumber slices, you can add taste. Drinking may become more enjoyable as a result. Pay attention to dehydration warning signs, such as dark urine or thirst, and act quickly by drinking water. Consider drinking beverages with electrolytes to replace lost minerals if you exercise vigorously or perspire a lot.

Drinking enough water, preparing wholesome meals, and selecting wise snacks are all essential parts of eating healthily for peak performance. You may make sure that your dietary decisions promote your general well-being and financial success by adopting these procedures into your daily routine.

Chapter 10
Fitness and Exercise for Entrepreneurs

Prioritizing physical health through regular exercise is crucial for achieving both financial fitness and well-being. This chapter looks into the many advantages of leading an active lifestyle, especially for busy entrepreneurs, and examines the relevance of adding exercise to your daily routine.

Photo by olia danilevich:

Chapter Ten

Exercise & Fitness for Entrepreneurs

Prioritizing physical health through regular exercise is crucial for achieving both financial fitness and well-being. What draws people to the gym? People go to the gym to exercise physically, increase their level of fitness, improve their health, reach specific fitness objectives, benefit from guided workouts, and have access to fitness equipment.

This chapter looks into the many advantages of leading an active lifestyle, especially for busy entrepreneurs, and examines the relevance of adding exercise to your daily routine.

Despite these difficulties, incorporating exercise into your daily routine is not only possible but also essential for good health and performance. Entrepreneurs frequently find themselves caught up in a maelstrom of duties and time restraints. Set aside certain times for exercise, just as you would meetings and professional assignments. Give your exercise appointments the same level of respect. Start with brief workouts if you're new to fitness or have a hectic schedule. Even only 20 to 30 minutes of exercise can have a big impact. Incorporating a variety of exercises, such as cardio workouts, weight training, yoga, or even walking meetings, will make exercise interesting.

If possible, use your lunch break for a quick workout. Whether it's a brisk walk, yoga stretches, or a quick bodyweight workout, it can re-energize you for the afternoon. Consider starting your day with a morning workout to boost your energy levels, improve focus, and set a positive tone for the day. Look into workouts you may do at your desk or in your workspace that are appropriate for the office. The sedentary nature of desk work can be countered with easy stretches or chair squats.

Types of exercise that might be suitable for your hectic schedule.

1. Interval training at a high intensity (HIIT):
Short bursts of intensive exercise are interspersed with rest intervals in HIIT. It is time-effective, can enhance general fitness in a short period, and has cardiovascular advantages.

2. Bodyweight Exercises
Exercises using only your body weight, such as push-ups, squats, lunges, and planks, require no special equipment and can be performed anywhere. They increase strength and endurance while working out several muscle groups.

3. Exercise Circuits:
By combining multiple exercises in a sequence, circuit training enables you to work on numerous muscle groups while maintaining an elevated heart rate. It's a quick and efficient approach to get a full-body workout.

4. Tabata Exercises:
Exercises at a high intensity are done for 20 seconds followed by 10 seconds of recovery during a tabata workout. They increase metabolism and cardiovascular fitness quickly yet effectively.

5. Stretching or yoga:
Yoga or stretching exercises can assist in increasing flexibility, ease tension in the muscles, and encourage relaxation. It benefits both physical and emotional health.

6. Quick cardio workouts
Short cardio exercises, including brisk walking, a fast jog, or jumping jacks, can help you maintain an active lifestyle even on hectic days and boost your cardiovascular system.

7. Workouts with Resistance Bands:
Resistance bands are adaptable and portable equipment for building strength. They can be

utilized to deliver an efficient workout while focusing on different muscle areas.

8. Scaling Stairs:
If you're in a building with multiple stories, think about using the stairs rather than the elevator. It's a quick and easy way to add cardio to your day.

9. Desk workouts:
Simple desk workouts like sitting leg lifts, seated marches, and sat twists can be done even while you're at work to stay in shape.

10. Walking Intervals
Take brief pauses throughout the day to go for walks. Walking for even a brief period can have a positive impact on your health.

The Benefits of Regular Exercise

Numerous advantages that go beyond physical fitness are provided by regular physical activity. Adopting an active lifestyle as a business owner or employee can improve your general health and increase your business savvy. Exercise promotes mental clarity, focus, and cognitive performance by increasing blood flow to the brain. It can help lessen the symptoms of stress, worry, and sadness. Exercise is a natural stress reliever that releases endorphins, which improve mood and lower stress. This is especially helpful for entrepreneurs who deal with high-pressure situations. Regular physical activity is linked to increased productivity and improves problem-solving, decision-making, and creative skills. Contrary to popular belief, exercise increases energy levels. Regular exercise also improves stamina and endurance, which will keep you attentive all day. A well-rested entrepreneur is more focused and capable of making wise decisions. Exercise helps to improve sleep quality. Regular exercise fosters healthier nutritional choices, more water intake, and less sedentary behavior, all of which contribute to adopting a healthier lifestyle overall.

Regular exercise lowers the likelihood of developing chronic illnesses like heart disease, diabetes, and obesity, which can result in fewer health-related setbacks on your entrepreneurial journey. Sports or group fitness activities can provide networking possibilities, and establishing connections with like-minded people can help your business. Regular exercise encourages you to take breaks from work and engage in activities that promote relaxation. It also cultivates discipline and goal-setting skills, which are immediately transferable to your entrepreneurial ventures. Regular exercise is an essential part of living a healthy life.

Creating a fitness plan

Being able to define specific fitness goals that are in line with your aspirations can help you be more productive every day. These goals could be things like enhancing your cardiovascular health, gaining strength, increasing flexibility, or reaching a certain level of physical endurance. A well-structured fitness plan is your road map to achieving your health and fitness goals as an entrepreneur. By evaluating your present level of fitness, you can establish your starting point and identify your strengths and potential improvement areas.
Choose physical activities that suit your preferences and your objectives. Running, cycling, weightlifting, swimming, yoga, and team sports are a few examples of this. Include workouts as non-negotiable appointments in your weekly plan, allot them specified times, and treat them with the same dedication as business meetings. To prevent plateaus and keep making progress, build progression into your exercise regimen by progressively raising the intensity, duration, or complexity of your workouts. To address overall

fitness, a well-rounded fitness program combines both aerobic (aerobic) and anaerobic (strength training) activities. Don't forget to include rest days and flexibility workouts as well; these activities, like yoga or stretching, improve mobility and lower the risk of injury.

To assist you in developing a personalized fitness plan based on your needs and goals, think about speaking with a fitness expert or personal trainer. They can inspire you and offer professional direction. Entrepreneurial schedules can be erratic, so be ready to modify your workout regimen as necessary. However, try to keep it intact even when you have a hectic week.

Staying Motivation

Although it can be difficult to stay motivated, doing so is essential for keeping up a regular workout schedule. Find Your "Why": Recognize the inner drive that drives you to exercise, comprehend why fitness is important to you personally, and how it relates to your long-term success and well-being. To stay motivated, break your exercise objectives down into smaller, more manageable benchmarks. Sharing your fitness aspirations with someone who can hold you accountable, such as a friend, partner, or mentor, can help you stay motivated. Join sports leagues, fitness programs, or online forums; the companionship and encouragement of others with similar interests help keep you motivated. To avoid getting bored during your workouts, mix things up by trying new things or checking out other fitness courses to keep your routine interesting. To track your workouts, progress, and new goals, keep a fitness notebook or use fitness monitoring apps. Establish a system of rewards for reaching your fitness targets, and when you do, treat yourself to something pleasurable or significant. Consider making exercise a part of your morning routine. Doing so can help you start the day off well and prevent you from skipping your workout because of other obligations. Reflect frequently on your fitness journey and recognize your accomplishments to increase motivation and self-worth.

As an entrepreneur, maintaining an active and healthy lifestyle requires developing a fitness plan and maintaining motivation. By setting clear goals, adopting a structured plan, and using motivational techniques, you can make sure that exercise becomes a regular part of your routine, enhancing both your physical health and your success as an entrepreneur.

Chapter 11
Annual Physical Check Up

What is the significance of visiting a doctor as a business owner?
Your ability to lead, create, and manage your business successfully depends heavily on how healthy you are as an entrepreneur or worker

Photo by olia danilevich:

Chapter Eleven

Annual Physical Examination

What is the significance of visiting a doctor as a business owner?

Your ability to lead, create, and manage your business successfully depends heavily on how healthy you are as an entrepreneur or worker. Regular doctor visits are essential for preserving your health and well-being, which can benefit your entrepreneurial endeavors. The following are some major justifications for why business owners should visit a doctor:

1. Early Health Issues Detection.
2. Wellness and prevention.
3. Stress reduction.
4. optimum physical condition.
5. Control of Long-Term Conditions.
6. Aid for mental health.
7. Work-Life Integration.
8. preventing issues with long-term health.
9. Make wise decisions.
10. modeling behavior.
11. Planning for Continuity.
12. Opportunities for Networking.

Entrepreneurs frequently devote a lot of time and energy to growing their companies, but it's crucial to remember to take care of your health as well. Regular doctor visits can help you maintain your physical and mental health, enabling you to face the opportunities and challenges of entrepreneurship with resiliency and success.

Benefits and Importance of Annual Medical Checkups

A thorough medical examination is performed by a healthcare practitioner during an annual medical check-up, often known as a routine health check or yearly physical. This examination is often advised for people of all ages to track their health status, identify any potential health problems early, and foster general well-being. Due to the particular demands and difficulties of their jobs, entrepreneurs in particular can gain a lot from yearly physicals. The following are some reasons why business owners should get yearly physicals:

Important of annual medical check up

Annual check-ups enable the early detection of health problems; catching problems in the early stages frequently results in more effective treatment and better outcomes. Routine check-ups also include screenings, vaccinations, and lifestyle advice that can aid in the prevention of chronic diseases. Annual check-ups assist in managing and monitoring pre-existing medical conditions to make sure they are under control if you have them. Doctors make use of patient checkups as an opportunity to inform patients about their health, respond to inquiries, and offer advice on healthy lifestyle options. Annual exams create a baseline for your health, enabling medical professionals to spot changes over time and adjust their recommendations accordingly. High levels of stress are common for business owners. The option to talk about stress management techniques and their effects on health is offered by routine checkups. Entrepreneurs must take care of their mental health. Exams might involve evaluations for depression, anxiety, and other mental health issues. Physical, mental, and emotional health are all evaluated during checkups, providing a thorough picture of your current state of health.

Benefits for Business Owners

Optimal cognitive function, decision-making abilities, and problem-solving abilities are all necessary for business success and are all supported by good health. Entrepreneurs can get suggestions on how to handle stress, lessen burnout, and keep a healthy work-life balance. Regular check-ups can aid in spotting burnout warning signs and offer preventative measures. By averting health problems that can later obstruct corporate operations, investing in health now can result in long-term success.

Exams offer a chance to talk about work-life balance and how to successfully preserve it. Entrepreneurs who are in good health are more able to face obstacles head-on and embrace opportunities. The danger of health-related disruptions to corporate operations is reduced by routine examinations. Making health a priority sets a good example for employees and fosters a culture of well-being throughout the business.

As an entrepreneur, scheduling annual physicals is an investment in both your health and the long-term success of your company. It enables you to take charge of your health, spot problems before they become serious, and get advice on how to strike a healthy balance between work and life. Keep in mind that your ability to lead, develop, and accomplish your entrepreneurial goals is strongly impacted by how you feel.

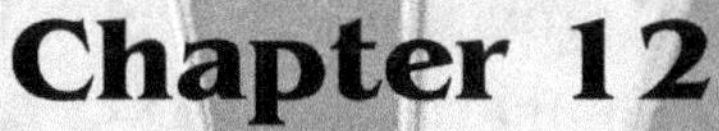

Chapter 12

Intentionality

making decisions and acting
with a clear knowledge of the
importance and desired results.
Beyond accidental or
haphazard behavior,
intentionality indicates a
careful and considered attitude
to navigating one's life,
relationships, and aspirations.

Chapters Twelve

Intentionality

The term "intentionality" describes how deliberate and purposeful actions, choices, and behaviors are. It entails deliberately making decisions and acting with a clear knowledge of the importance and desired results. Beyond accidental or haphazard behavior, intentionality indicates a careful and considered attitude to navigating one's life, relationships, and aspirations.

In the context of entrepreneurship, intentionality refers to the process of establishing precise objectives, developing well-defined strategies, and coming to conclusions that are in line with both your overall well-being and the larger vision of the company. Intentional business owners are proactive in looking for possibilities, taking reasonable risks, and making sure that their deeds support the expansion and success of their companies. Let's discuss the essential components of intentionality.

Clarity of Purpose: Knowing one's purpose, objectives, and values. Entrepreneurs who are deliberate in their business decisions are motivated by a clear understanding of their motivations and how they hope to have a significant influence.

Clarity of purpose is that you need to understand your motivations for following a given objective, course of action, or activity clearly and in detail. Knowing your fundamental reasons, values, and the influence you hope to have is necessary. People are motivated and directed in their activities, choices, and efforts when they have a clear sense of purpose. In entrepreneurship, purposefulness is essential.

Making Intentional Decisions: Intentional decisions are not hasty or reactionary. They have been carefully considered, taking into account the facts at hand, any negative effects, and how well they correspond with long-term objectives.

Making choices that are in line with your goals, values, and desired outcomes requires careful and deliberate thought. It entails spending time evaluating the available information, balancing advantages and disadvantages, and foreseeing various outcomes before making a decision. Beyond acting on impulse, thoughtful decision-making ensures that choices are well-founded and well-justified. Entrepreneurship requires making deliberate decisions.

Focus and Direction: Intentional people keep their attention on their goals and stay away from distractions that will hinder them. They can successfully manage their time, resources, and energy thanks to this focus.

Entrepreneurship is centered on focus and direction, which steer actions, choices, and strategies toward achieving particular objectives. They entail keeping an accurate perspective of what must be completed and directing efforts with purpose and tenacity. Focus and direction are crucial components of the entrepreneurial environment:

Focus:

Focus is the act of focusing one's attention, effort, and resources on a certain task, target, or goal. Focused business owners are less prone to be sidetracked by pursuits that don't advance their principal objectives. Focus increases performance, reduces waste, and maximizes the effect of actions.

Priority of Focus:

Efficiency: By concentrating their energies on things that advance advancement, entrepreneurs can work more effectively. It cuts down on time lost on pointless pursuits.

Prioritization: Focus helps business owners rank tasks and projects according to their significance and compatibility with long-term goals.

Quality: Because entrepreneurs give the task at hand their entire attention and competence, focused efforts produce higher-quality output.

Reduced Distractions: Entrepreneurs who are focused are better able to fend off sidetrackers that could impede their growth and pursuit of goals.

Goal Achievement: Entrepreneurs who take a concentrated approach make steady progress toward their objectives.

Direction:

A defined path and purpose for where the entrepreneurial journey is going are referred to as having direction. Entrepreneurs with a clear sense of purpose are aware of their long-term goals, their mission, and the measures necessary to get there. Making decisions and plotting a course for advancement is made easier with the help of direction.

The significance of direction

Direction offers advice for decision-making, ensuring that business owners make decisions that are in line with their long-term objectives.

Entrepreneurs who have a clear direction are more motivated and determined because they understand why they are working so hard.

Consistency: Direction encourages consistency in activities and methods, keeping business owners from deviating from their intended path.

Adaptation: Even when conditions change, entrepreneurs may make adjustments while adhering to their main goal when they have a clear path.

Direction aids business owners in keeping a long-term perspective and making decisions that support sustainable growth.

In conclusion, the factors that propel entrepreneurship ahead are direction and focus. Focus makes ensuring that efforts are centered on tasks that advance goals, while direction gives progress the meaning and path it needs. These ideas enable business owners to make deliberate choices, increase productivity, and realize their goals.

Intentionality incorporates mindfulness, which occurs when people are fully present and involved in what they are doing. Every activity has a purpose and advances the goals of the individual.

In the context of entrepreneurship, mindful actions are defined as taking actions, making decisions, and interacting with others while maintaining a high level of awareness, presence, and intentionality. It entails being fully present in the moment, realizing the importance of every action, and making deliberate decisions that are consistent with one's values, objectives, and the venture's overall vision. Entrepreneurial attempts are greatly influenced by the nature, significance, and success of our acts.

Adaptability with Intention: Entrepreneurs are aware of the value of adaptability while also being deliberate. They remain flexible and willing to change course as required, always keeping their ultimate goal in mind.

Entrepreneurs who are capable of adapting to changes, difficulties, and uncertainties while staying true to their overall vision and goals are said to be doing so with purpose. It entails retaining a strong sense of direction and intentionality while remaining adaptable and receptive to adjustments. A key quality that enables entrepreneurs to thrive in the face of change in the entrepreneurial world is the ability to adapt with purpose.

Personal Development: Intentionality encompasses personal growth. Self-reflection, continual improvement, and active skill and knowledge development are all characteristics of intentional entrepreneurs.

By offering a planned and concentrated approach to self-improvement and development, intentionality plays a vital part in human progress. People who behave intentionally and actively focus their behaviors, choices, and efforts toward predetermined objectives and ideals. This methodical strategy encourages self-awareness, learning, and transformation, which results in significant personal progress. Here are some ways that intentionality promotes personal development:

Effective communication requires that messages be delivered with precision, openness, and respect for others' feelings. Entrepreneurs who deliberately communicate make sure that their messages reflect their goals and core beliefs.

A key component of both personal and professional success is effective communication. It entails effectively and communicating thoughts, feelings, and facts to others. In the context of entrepreneurship, excellent communication is essential for developing trusting connections, encouraging teamwork, and realizing corporate objectives. Here is a closer examination of the components and advantages of good communication:

Value-Driven Relationships: Entrepreneurs intentionally cultivate relationships with people who share their values and who help their businesses succeed. Over transactional encounters, they place more value on genuine friendships.

Relationships that are motivated by shared values, respect for one another, and a desire to make meaningful connections are cultivated via intentionality, which is essential. When people approach relationships with intention, they place a high emphasis on open communication, being real, and developing partnerships that are consistent with their beliefs. In the world of entrepreneurship, intentionality in connections produces more profound alliances, teams, and encounters. To foster connections that are value-driven, intentionality can do the following:

Long-Term Vision: Intentional entrepreneurs make decisions based on a long-term vision. They ensure that short-term advantages do not jeopardize their long-term objectives by taking into account how their decisions will affect both the present and the future.

Intentionality has enormous effects on a long-term vision in entrepreneurship and can greatly influence the course and success of a venture. Achieving certain objectives through deliberate and purposeful behavior is what is meant by intentionality. Intentionality increases the influence of a long-term vision by ensuring that every action is in line with the project's main aims and objectives. The results of intentionality on a long-term vision are as follows:

A deliberate and goal-driven attitude to activities and decisions is what is meant by intentionality. Clear objectives, considered approaches, and a dedication to making decisions that are consistent with one's principles and long-term objectives serve as the compass for entrepreneurs who conduct their business with intention. Entrepreneurs can negotiate obstacles, seize opportunities, and make a real impact both within their businesses and outside of them thanks to this thoughtful approach.

Chapter 13

achieving financial freedom

The foundation of the trip we've been on throughout this book is aching a financial freedom and a sound health.

Chapter Thirteenth

Achieving Financial Freedom

The foundation of the trip we've been on throughout this book is financial freedom. We'll examine important methods for achieving financial freedom in this chapter, such as sensible saving and investing as well as creating passive income sources. These tactics play a crucial role in helping you safeguard your financial future and live the life you want.

1. Methods for Efficient Saving and Investing

Start by creating a thorough budget that details your income and costs. This budget acts as a road map for managing your money successfully, allowing you to keep tabs on your spending and pinpoint areas where you may make savings or spending reductions. Establish your long- and short-term financial objectives. Having specific objectives gives your financial efforts incentive and direction, whether they be supporting your children's school, preparing for retirement, or saving for a down payment on a home. Saving three to six months' worth of living expenses in a liquid and easily accessible account should be the aim, building an emergency fund is crucial, when unforeseen occurrences like job loss or medical difficulties occur, this fund serves as a financial safety net.

Make paying off high-interest debt, like credit card bills, a priority because it can deplete your financial resources. Create a plan to gradually reduce and pay off your debt.

To reduce risk and maximize profits, diversify your investment holdings. Depending on your risk appetite and time horizon, you may want to mix stocks, bonds, real estate, and other assets in your portfolio. Contributions to retirement plans like 401(k)s and IRAs should be increased. Utilize employer-sponsored retirement plans, particularly if your company matches your contributions. When investing in the stock market, use the dollar-cost-averaging technique, which entails making monthly fixed-amount investments and can help lessen the impact of market volatility. Stay informed about economic developments, tax regulations, and investment opportunities while continuing your education in personal finance and investment methods. To develop a customized investing strategy that is in line with your objectives and risk tolerance, think about speaking with a financial advisor or planner.

2. Creating Streams of Passive Income

You can invest in rental properties, real estate investment trusts (REITs), or real estate crowdfunding platforms to get passive income from real estate. Invest in dividend-paying companies, which offer recurring dividend income that can be reinvested or used as cash flow. Create and market original works of art. Consider monetizing your creative or intellectual assets by turning them into e-books, licensing your pictures, or creating money-making online courses if you have them. Start an online venture that can make money from advertising, affiliate marketing, or product sales, such as an e-commerce site, blog, or YouTube channel. To earn more interest on your funds than you would with conventional savings accounts, look into high-yield savings accounts or certificates of deposit (CDs). You can rent out equipment, vehicles, or storage space in addition to real estate to make passive revenue. If you are talented in the arts or music, royalties from songs, books, or artwork can help you sustain a living.

Some businesses provide DRIPs, which enable you to compound your investment over time by reinvesting dividends into additional shares of stock.

Think about annuities, which are financial products that offer consistent payments in return for a lump-sum initial investment. Annuities can offer a steady income stream during retirement.

3. Continuously Educating Yourself

It is essential to commit to ongoing financial education: Stay current on financial news, market trends, and economic indicators that could impact your investments and financial decisions. Financial markets, investment opportunities, and economic landscapes are dynamic and constantly changing. Read books, articles, and blogs produced by financial professionals to gain a deeper understanding of personal finance, investing methods, and economic theories. Consider going to financial workshops, webinars, and seminars that provide information on many facets of financial planning and investing. Consult with financial planners or advisors if necessary so they may offer you individualized advice and knowledge based on your financial status and objectives. Explore areas like taxation, retirement planning, estate planning, and risk management to broaden your knowledge of finance. Participate in local or online financial forums, communities, and discussion groups where you may exchange ideas, pick the brains of others, and post queries. Recognize your financial shortcomings and missteps, and draw the lessons you can from them to inform your future choices. By comprehending ideas like compound interest, asset allocation, risk tolerance, and the effectiveness of long-term investing, you may improve your financial literacy. Keep in mind that by improving your abilities and earning potential, investing in your personal and professional growth can also have a positive financial impact.

4. Reviewing and Modifying Your Financial Goals

Financial objectives should change as your life circumstances, desires, and economic environment do. Staying on the path to financial freedom requires routinely examining and revising your financial goals. Your long-term financial objectives can be divided into smaller, more attainable milestones, allowing you to monitor your progress and recognize accomplishments. Assessing whether your financial goals are still relevant and realistic requires regular reviews, ideally once a year. Adjustments to your financial goals may be necessary as a result of significant life events like marriage, parenthood, professional changes, or unanticipated financial gains.

Be ready to modify your goals in reaction to changes in your financial condition brought on by economic downturns, inflation, and interest rate adjustments. Your risk tolerance might change as you move closer to financial freedom; as a result, you should review your investment portfolio and techniques to make sure they are in line with your new risk tolerance. Review your emergency savings and insurance to be sure they're still sufficient in case of unforeseen setbacks. Consider aspects including your target retirement age, lifestyle expectations, and anticipated lifespan as you reevaluate your retirement savings goals.

Reevaluate your income objectives as your job develops and take into account any new prospects for investing and saving. Maintain a healthy balance between your money ambitions and your entire well-being; your financial objectives should enhance your general sense of fulfillment and happiness.

You can stay flexible in your quest for financial freedom by always learning new things and frequently reviewing and changing your financial goals. By being flexible, you may adjust to shifting conditions in a way that keeps you on the right track for a prosperous and meaningful future.

In the last chapters, we'll look at ways to manage stress, find a work-life balance, and practice holistic well-being, all of which will help you on your path to financial security, personal fulfillment, and good health. With the help of these realizations, you'll be able to live a balanced life that combines material achievement with all-around well-being and satisfaction.

Chapter 14
Sustaining A Balanced Life

Maintaining a balanced existence becomes crucial in our drive for financial independence and profound well-being. This chapter emphasizes the importance of routine check-ins and the capacity to make the required adjustments to maintain equilibrium in the face of life's always-shifting demands.

Chapter Fourteen

Sustaining A Balanced Life

Maintaining a balanced existence becomes crucial in our drive for financial independence and profound well-being. This chapter emphasizes the importance of routine check-ins and the capacity to make the required adjustments to maintain equilibrium in the face of life's always-shifting demands.

1. Regularly Check In

We all know it's important to regularly check in with yourself and your life priorities to stay on course. So set aside some time for self-reflection to assess your current state of balance and reflect on your goals, values, and what truly matters to you. Maintaining a balanced life is similar to steering a ship through constantly shifting waters. Check-in on your financial and personal objectives from time to time to see if they still reflect your beliefs and aspirations and are doable. What are your top objectives in life—family, health, work, personal growth, and financial security—and do you give them the attention they require? Check your energy levels and general health to see whether you're showing any symptoms of burnout, stress, or physical exhaustion. Recognize the value of rejuvenation and self-care. Examine the health of your relationships with your loved ones, friends, and coworkers. Do you still value them or have you neglected them as a result of your work or money goals? Examine your work-life balance; do you spend too much time working at the expense of your personal life, or the opposite? Strive for a balance that benefits both.

Regularly assess your financial situation. Are you achieving your financial objectives without compromising other facets of your life? Are there indications of financial hardship or excessive spending?

Think about tracking your total life satisfaction, happiness, and stress levels using well-being measurements. Insights can be gained by using tools like the Perma Model (Positive Emotion, Engagement, Relationships, Meaning, Accomplishment).

2. Making Changes to Keep the Balance

Life balance is an ongoing effort that calls for adaptability and the readiness to change course when necessary. Make sure that self-care is still an essential component of your daily routine. Spend time doing things that will refresh your mind, body, and spirit.

Set up clear boundaries between your personal and professional lives. To safeguard your time and well-being, let your coworkers, clients, and family members know about these boundaries.

At work, delegate jobs and contract out duties as much as you can. By doing this, you might have more time for more crucial tasks in your personal and professional life. Recognize when a commitment or opportunity doesn't fit with your values or objectives and learn to say no. Give the things that make you happy and fulfilled top priority. Invest in time-management techniques that work to increase productivity while working and free up more time for personal development, family time, and leisure activities. Recognize that quality time spent with loved ones is more important than quantity, and try to make every contact meaningful and gratifying by being there. Make sure your financial goals are still on track by conducting frequent evaluations, and if required, adapt your financial plans to reflect shifting conditions. Recognize that different periods of life may necessitate varying degrees of concentration on different priorities; be adaptable in adjusting to these stages while maintaining overall balance. Consider obtaining advice from a therapist, counselor, or life coach if you find it difficult to keep your equilibrium or make the necessary changes. Commit to reviewing your life balance frequently. This process should be ongoing so that you can reassess when your circumstances change.

Maintaining a balanced life is a journey, not a destination. It calls for a dedication to self-awareness, the capacity to give priority to what matters, and the bravery to modify course when necessary. You can live a harmonious existence that integrates financial success with general well-being and enjoyment by doing regular check-ins and remaining flexible.

3. celebrating successes

It's simple to lose sight of our successes and advancements along the way as we relentlessly pursue financial prosperity and well-being. It's important to acknowledge accomplishments, no matter how modest, for various reasons:

Recognizing your successes helps you stay motivated by reinforcing the idea that your efforts are paying off and motivating you to keep going.

Celebrations stimulate gratitude, prompt you to reflect on what you've accomplished, and foster a sense of happiness and appreciation. They serve as positive reinforcement for your actions and choices and serve to remind you that your journey is defined by accomplishments, not just obstacles. The celebration of these milestones gives you a sense of direction and progress. Achievements frequently represent important turning points in your journey.

4. Avoiding Typical Mistakes

Maintaining a balanced existence has its own set of difficulties and potential traps; being aware of these common roadblocks will help you travel more successfully. Overworking might result from the constant pursuit of financial achievement. Establishing and upholding clear boundaries for work hours will help you avoid this. Maintaining balance necessitates self-care; failing to do so can cause burnout and impair your general well-being. Financial objectives are vital, but concentrating only on money might cause one to overlook other crucial facets of life, such as relationships and health. Focus on your journey rather than constantly comparing yourself to others, especially in terms of financial achievement, as this can cause worry and discontent.

A balanced existence depends on strong connections; disregarding them in the name of monetary gain might result in loneliness and misery.

Prioritize your physical and mental health to ensure that you have the vigor and energy to achieve your goals. A journey might be hampered by disregarding signals of stress, worry, or despair. Mental health is just as important as physical health. Goals that are firmly adhered to without regular evaluation risk becoming out of sync with your changing priorities. it can be embraced as a learning opportunity and a stepping stone toward achievement, but it can also paralyze growth.

It takes attentiveness, adaptability, and a dedication to recognizing accomplishments while avoiding typical pitfalls to strike a balance between material success and holistic well-being. You can live a harmonious existence that merges financial wealth with general well-being and enjoyment by remaining aware of your inner compass and constantly checking your balance.

In the final chapter, we'll summarize the most important ideas from this book and give you a road map for starting your journey toward financial independence, health, and a satisfying life.

Conclusion

We have been searching for something remarkable as we have read through the pages of "Financial Fitness: Balancing Health and Wealth for Entrepreneurs and All Workers": the seamless fusion of financial fitness with healthy living. As we draw to a close, it's important to consider the main ideas, offer support for your ongoing journey, and offer some closing comments on finding balance.

Recap of Important Points

We have unearthed a plethora of ideas, tactics, and insights for fostering both financial fitness and a healthy lifestyle throughout this book.

Financial fitness includes careful financial planning, wise investing, and living within one's means in addition to wealth accumulation. Achieving financial success should not jeopardize your physical or emotional health; rather, it should enhance them.

Understanding Your Financial Health, the first steps are to evaluate your existing financial condition, create clear financial goals, make a budget, keep track of your spending, and accumulate an emergency fund.

Building a Strong Financial Foundation, key elements of financial fitness which include managing debt, setting aside money for retirement, investing properly, diversifying your portfolio, and being aware of your risk tolerance.

The Relationship Between Financial Health and Physical Health such as Stress related to finances which can significantly affect your physical health. Budgeting wisely, managing debt, and keeping emergency funds on hand are all ways to lessen financial stress.

Mental health is important since it affects physical and mental health. Put stress reduction first, ask for help when you need it, and engage in mindfulness exercises. Exercise in Daily Life, physical activity improves overall health, mental clarity, and productivity, even with a busy schedule, find methods to fit exercise into your daily routine.

Your working space is very important so designing an Ergonomic Workspace, Managing Work-Life Balance, and Putting Strategies Into Practice To Prevent Burnout And Benefit From Regular Breaks. For small business owners looking to maximize productivity, time management, prioritizing, delegating, and using technology are crucial.

Financial Fitness for Small Business Owners. Successful entrepreneurship requires the management of business finances, the separation of personal and business money, the acquisition of business insurance, growth planning, and the navigating of taxation and legal problems.

Nutrition is essential for mental acuity, energy, and eating well for optimal performance. Create a food plan, choose your snacks wisely, and maintain a healthy hydration level.

Fitness & Exercise for Entrepreneurs, exercise should be a regular part of your routine, and you should be aware of the advantages of consistent physical activity. To get physically fit, make a personalized fitness plan by establishing clear goals and progressively increasing the intensity of your workouts.

How do you Stay Motivated? To stay dedicated to your fitness objectives, find internal motivation. You may also set milestones, involve others, and monitor your progress.

Gaining Financial independence. The secrets to gaining financial independence are strategies for prudent saving and investing, creating passive income sources, constantly educating yourself, and examining and revising financial goals. Maintaining a Balanced Life, keeping your life in balance requires regular check-ins, making adjustments, acknowledging your successes, and avoiding frequent mistakes.

Motivating YOU to Aim for Financial Fitness and Healthy Living

I want to give you some words of encouragement as you finish this part of our trip, It takes a lifetime commitment to pursue financial stability and a healthy lifestyle. It's a route paved with difficulties, victories, setbacks, and deep development moments. Accept the adventure with tenacity and a firm conviction that you can design the life you want.

Keep in mind that every small step you take toward achieving financial stability and a healthy lifestyle counts. Be kind to yourself, enjoy your successes, and absorb lessons from them. When necessary, seek out assistance from friends, family, mentors, or experts. There are tools and communities ready to support and elevate you on this journey, so you are not traveling alone.

Last Words on Finding Balance

The goal of working toward both financial fitness and a healthy lifestyle is balance. It is the art of balancing your goals, commitments, and wants in a way that fosters happiness, success, and prosperity. Balance is a dynamic equilibrium that requires continual monitoring and adjustment; it is not static.

Keep in mind that finding balance is a highly individual adventure as you travel the challenging terrain of modern life. You might have a different definition of balance than others, and that's just acceptable. Honor your principles, follow your inner compass, and embrace your journey.

You can create a life of meaning, passion, and abundance via this pursuit of balance. May your journey be characterized by a great sense of well-being, financial independence, good health, and fulfilling relationships. Keep on because your fortitude and perseverance are demonstrated by the adventure itself.

I appreciate you coming along with me on this exploration. I wish you success and happiness as you turn the page and begin your road to achieving financial stability, good health, and a well-balanced existence. Your adventure is waiting for you, and the opportunities are endless.

lives. We work hard to establish businesses, advance in our careers, and accumulate riches. Although having financial security is vital, we occasionally forget about another crucial component of our well-being: our health.

In "Financial Fitness: Balancing Health and Wealth for Lasting Prosperity," we set out on a transformational journey that questions traditional ideas of prosperity. This book is not simply about money; it is about striking a healthy and long-lasting balance between material success and overall well-being.

We are used to establishing lofty goals and working incredibly hard to attain them as businesspeople, professionals, and people who like to get things done. But what if there was an alternative route, one that brought about not only material success but also good health, emotional fortitude, and a sense of direction? What if we could achieve financial success without compromising our health, and vice versa?

We examine the complex relationship between our financial situation and our physical health in the pages that follow. We explore the fundamental relationship between the two and learn that taking care of both facets of our lives is necessary for obtaining true success.

"Financial Fitness" leads you on a journey of self-discovery through interesting anecdotes, helpful counsel, and doable techniques. You'll discover how to:

Learn how financial decisions affect your health and well-being and how to make decisions that are consistent with your beliefs and goals by reading Balance the Budget of Your Life.

Consider the value of physical and mental wellness as the cornerstone of long-term prosperity by investing in your health. Discover how making health investments pays off in all facets of life.

Develop Financial Resilience: Learn how to strengthen your finances so that you can withstand life's financial storms without jeopardizing your well-being.

Discover Your Purpose: Recognize the part that passion and purpose play in your financial and personal path, and how they can result in a richer and more fulfilling life.

"Financial Fitness" is more than simply a book; it's a guide to living a balanced life. It serves as a reminder that true prosperity includes both money and happiness. A new paradigm of success is being offered, one in which you may have it all—financial stability, thriving health, and a life full of meaning and joy.

Join us as we investigate the relationship between health and money and set out on a route to long-term success as we go on this transforming adventure. It's time to rethink what success means and to create a life that is not just financially prosperous but also abundant in health, joy, and fulfillment.

Getting Long-Term Prosperity

In "Financial Fitness: Balancing Health and Wealth for Lasting Prosperity," we have taken a deep look at how our financial and physical well-being are intertwined. We have learned that true prosperity is a symphony of health, purpose, and financial security rather than the sole pursuit of cash. Let's take a moment to consider the most important things we've learned and the way forward as we come to the end of this transforming trip.

A Harmonious Symphony: Throughout this book, we have discovered that our health and happiness do not have to be sacrificed in the name of pursuing financial success. Instead, these components work together in harmony to strengthen one another. Our lives find harmony in the balance of monetary security, strong health, and a feeling of purpose, just as a symphony depends on the ideal balance of instruments.

The Power of Balance: Making informed decisions and intentional choices are necessary to balance the budget of our life. We can match our financial objectives with our beliefs, making sure that every dollar we spend, invest, or save advances our overall well-being.

Investing in Ourselves: We've talked about how important it is to take care of our health because it is the basis for long-term prosperity. When we place a high priority on our physical and mental health, we not only protect our future but also improve our experiences in the here and now.

Financial Resilience: During our trip, we learned how important financial resilience is. By strengthening our financial roots, we equip ourselves to face life's challenges without compromising our well-being or sense of well-being.

Passion and Purpose: A fulfilling existence depends on the presence of passion and purpose, which are not frills. We can imbue our endeavors with meaning as business owners, professionals, and people looking to flourish. This will direct us toward a richer and more fulfilling life.

Accepting a New Paradigm: To conclude, let's accept this new theory of success, which goes beyond the conventional definitions of riches and considers the virtually limitless potential of all-encompassing affluence. Let's commit to creating lives that are abundant in health, pleasure, and fulfillment in addition to being financially secure.

Let us keep in mind that the path to enduring wealth is still being traveled when we leave these pages and enter the real world. It is a way of life, not a goal, where happiness is the true test of success, where wealth and health coexist in perfect harmony, and where every activity is driven by a sense of purpose.

May the knowledge imparted in this book act as a lighthouse for you as you travel the road to riches. May you discover the harmony you desire, the health you value, and the wealth to realize your aspirations. Above all, may you learn that true prosperity is a lifelong journey that is filled with joy, purpose, and the rich tapestry of a life well lived, rather than a destination.

Here's to your continued success and the amazing opportunities that lay ahead